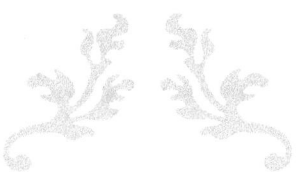

Models Stop Traffic

How to Dodge Enslavement in Pursuit of Your Dream to Become the Next Top Model

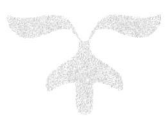

Airica D. Kraehmer

Based on a True Story

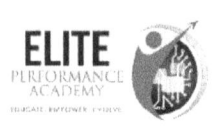 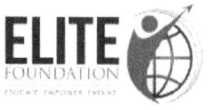 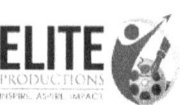

MISSION STATEMENT

Elite Educates and Empowers Survivors to Evolve into Thriving-Leaders, to Find Their Voice and become Warriors of Change.

EliteFundsFreedom.org   #ItEndsWithUs   #EndHT

Copyright © 2018 Elite Foundation Publisher®

All rights reserved. No part of this book may be used or reproduced in any manner whatsoever without prior written consent of the author, except as provided by the Unites States of America copyright law.

Published by Elite Foundation Publisher®, Ft. Lauderdale, FL.

Edited by: Mr. Erick Vera

Cover Art Designed by: Mr. Jesus Cordero

Elite Foundation Publisher® is a registered trademark.

Printed in the United States of America.

ISBN-13: 978-1732077829

This publication is designed to provide accurate and authoritative information regarding the subject matter covered. It is sold with the understanding that the publisher is not engaged in rendering legal, accounting, clinical or other professional advice. If legal advice or other expert assistance is required, the services of a competent professional should be sought. The opinions expressed by the authors in this book are not endorsed by Elite Foundation Publisher® and are the sole responsibility of the author rendering the opinion.

Most Elite Foundation Publisher® titles are available for bulk purchases for sales promotions, premiums, fundraising, and educational use. Special versions or book excerpts can also be created on direct request for specific needs aligned with Elite.

For more information, please write: info@EliteFundsFreedom.org

2003 West Cypress Creek Road, Ste. 103 Ft. Lauderdale, Florida 33369

Or email: ElitePublisher@EliteFundsFreedom.org

Visit us online at:

https://eliteperformanceacademy.us/elite-book-creation-publishing-services/

FOREWORD

In an age of discovery for humanity, we strive to excel and achieve excellence. Our advancements have led to new ways of doing, seeing, hearing and even to experiencing alternate realities.

Every gain heightens our abilities, refines our skills and we evolve.

International Bestselling Author Airica D. Kraehmer a Warrior of Change, survivor-leader contributes valuable context about the landscape within which human exploitation can flourish in **Models Stop Traffic.**

Now a 200,000,000.00-dollar criminal industry Human Trafficking is ravishing our vulnerable internationally and domestically in our own backyards virtually unseen.

Through the pages of this autobiographical retelling of the events that led to decisions a young, beautiful aspiring woman, should never have to make, simply because of a desire to pursue a dream, Airica teaches of vulnerabilities that can lead to unspeakable truths.

Airica now living in awareness, in pursuit of being an acclaimed Actor, is silent no more.

She transparently leads the reader through a discovery of what aspiring agency models can go through, when they are not adequately aware of the potential of being tricked and entrapped in the very environment they so very much want to break into seeking success.

Airica gently pulls back the veil to an under-ground world that exists within the modeling industry. An industry that has ushered in young vibrant beautiful women the likes of Gisele Bündchen, Heidi Klum, Adriana Francesca Lima, Alessandra Corine, Ambrósio and many others from all parts of the world, seeking discovery and the spotlight.

Airica's admiration for the elite standards of the industry remain intact, through her use of language, she draws you into the pictures formulated in her memory that tell her story of how she escaped from a coveted model house in New York City, seemingly prominent agent representation and the unknowing collusion of legitimate gigs, when so many of her model-sisters did not.

Airica now lives her higher purpose to illuminate her experienced atrocities and the pathway to achieve dreams, while being intentionally aware of possible realities;

- ❖ The reality that everything that looks too good to be true, sometimes isn't;
- ❖ The reality that the qualities most sought after in the industry are the very same predators seek;

❖ The reality that every subculture has its tell-signs and when you are seeking acceptance, it's imperative to your survivor that you learn these risk indicators.

The bravery of this young lady is a testament not only for aspiring models to model, it is a call to action for all of us, to be vigilant, actively observant and proactively aware of the insidious criminal injustice that exists in all industries, in every community, and unfortunately among people we may hold in high esteem.

Airica living in truth that she is precious, unconditionally loved and cherished, now knows the vulnerabilities that led her to be tricked, trapped and enslaved.

She was one of the fortunate ones who escaped. She tells that she will never forget her learnings, the lost and will use it to educate and empower aspiring models and actors to prevent them from ever experiencing these atrocities in an industry she holds dear.

Models Stop Traffic will have you clinging to each word on the page, envisioning, with vivid detail, the author's journey to salvation and freedom. Inspirational!

Onward and upward,
Jessica L. Vera, PhD,
Founder, Elite Foundation

"This is a well written and captivating read. The main character's experience is an eye opener, but what most of the public doesn't understand, is common. I would highly advise anyone interested in entering the modeling or fashion industry read this and will take away knowledge of how to protect themselves or a loved one. I think it's important for the people to know what models go through and it isn't just about the glam and the runway and flashing lights. It is hard work, and on your way to the top, there are people that will attempt to take advantage of you. This eye-opening story will hopefully bring awareness to those who have wanted to be a part of this industry. I have been a model for just under a decade and was fortunate enough to not go through this extreme situation, but it is a reality that needs to be stopped. It is imperative these issues be brought out to light often and it is an absolute necessity to educate the public through stories and sharing of these experiences."

Hana Young, Agency Model, Business Broker/Commercial Realtor, Director of Operations of Recovery Residences

---

Models Stop Traffic is an eye opening, non-fiction account of life altering events that took place during the main character, Daniellé Winters, pursuit of being a successful model. The author, Airica Kraehmer, eloquently details the passions that drive a young woman to achieve her dreams, which consequently make her vulnerable, and somewhat blind, to the unnerving demands of a dark subculture found within the industry.

From the opening paragraph, Airica can engage the reader as though they are witnessing Danielié Winters emotions and desires for attention. Each character begins to come to life, and it becomes difficult to find a point at which to stop reading.

The challenge in bringing recognition to the world of Human Trafficking is most difficult because we generally choose to not acknowledge its existence. Mostly because it is filled with tragedies too disgusting to understand. Airica rises above this challenge with great skill in detailing the thoughts and aspirations of a young woman, leading up to the moment of vulnerability.

Review by - **Dennis Lauchner**, Vice Chairman, CSS, Inc.

Reading stories from those who have not been through modern day slavery is life changing. But reading an autobiographical testimony is life altering. I felt like I was in Daniellé's shoes. Feeling her pain was an honor, even though I have gone through something similar but different myself. **Models Stop Traffic** is authentic and raw. It is respectful story written by a lady whose heart was broken, but not enough to give up her fighting.

This book also serves to reminder us how real and secretive modern-day slavery continues to be in our backyards.

This book has given me hope and encouragement to see someone who has experienced some of what I have and still desires to help others. It has inspired and motivated me in my healing process. It's easy to give up and feel down when healing. But when I see someone who does struggle and never gives up... It becomes my fuel to my fire.

Review by- **Lena Vera**, Human Trafficking Survivor

Airica D. Kraehmer, the author of **Models Stop Traffic** has spoken through the lenses of her truth and that of other girls, boys and women trapped in the world of facade and trickery.

The literary Imaginary in this book was insatiable.

You will travel with her to new places, good and bad places and unspeakable places; every embarkation was a destination you may have been time and time again; abused placed and the tricked places and maybe said nothing, did nothing and at times felt like nothing.

Airica, carefully crafted this masterpiece so you will experience the moments in real time; in some cases, your mind will be in the behind the camera with her.

A must read as the author gives the secret passage ways to a hidden life of trauma that can be the death of life or a life of death

Mothers see your little girls, beauty and poise; it should never be her entry to exploitation; leaving scars on her heart.

Exceptional World Changing Work!

Review by -**Grace L. Holden**, M.S. Counseling, Author of Dirty the journey from Victim to Victor and International Bestseller of Invincible, CEO Real Champions League

---

Models Stop Traffic had my attention and brought me into the story like if I had been waiting my whole life to read it. The author's every description of how Daniellé Winter's felt made me feel like I personally knew her. I was also intrigued by her past and present life's journey and excited yet also anxious about her future in The Big Apple. I look forward to reading the entire book and believe that this book is for 'such a time as this' for a new generation to understand that evil existence in our world and we must learn how to make positive choices and be a true friend to others even when the truth hurts.

Review by- **Tomas J. Lares**, Founder/CEO Florida Abolitionist, Inc.

Dedication

This is for the ones without a voice, the ones without a chance, the ones that lost hope long ago, the ones who keep praying and fighting, the ones who are now free, and the ones that died fighting. Please know, I carry you with me. You are not alone, nor forgotten, but loved with all my heart.

Contents

FOREWORD iii

Dedication x

Prologue: Lights! Camera! Wait. Back to One! 1

Section One: Glamour 6

Just Around the Bend 7

We've Only Just Begun 31

Call My Name 41

Glam 48

Birthdays 57

Section Two: Go-See 81

Lighted, Magnifying Mirror 82

Long Island. Quick Changes. 89

Brave 103

Lights. Camera. Action. 115

Backfire 134

Fight or Flight 139

If You Can Make It in New York 149

Section Three: Red Flags 161

Commencing Eventuality 162

Fashion Affliction 174

Buy Out 181

Don't Caress Fire 184

A Model's "Dream" 185

Human 196

Section Four: Covergirl 202

Thy Will Be Done 203

Acknowledgements 209

AUTHOR: AIRICA D KRAEHMER 211

Contact Information: 213

Prologue: Lights! Camera! Wait. Back to One!

It is like being five-years-old again dressed in the pink ball gown as the flower girl prancing down the aisle of your aunt's wedding. It is the thrill of a Girl Scout troop slumber party playing dress-up, pretending to be anything their hearts desire: princesses, physicians, or engineers. It is like having a professional makeup artist transform a teenage girl into being the dazzling prom queen. It is like the grace and poise of a flawlessly stunning bride on her wedding day. Herein lies one of the rooted drives behind womanhood.

Women are inspired by beauty. From a young age, females have the desire to be beautiful and create more beauty in the world. They paint their nails, perm their hair, diet for weight loss, read every self-help book, and watch dozens of YouTube beauty tutorials. Their rewards come in the form of compliments and societal approval of their new designer shoes. "Likes" add up on social media, and suddenly they are beauty bloggers and Instagram icons.

Some of them lucky enough to be in societal judgement of genetic favor, like Daniellé Winters, become fashion models. The mesmerizing chandelier hanging in a golden ballroom gives off the feeling of being on a fashion show runway. The mesmerizing sensation of seeing the bright lights of Times Square New York for the first time is the same sensation as the camera lights of a beauty campaign. For Daniellé this was reality, and it was that mesmerizing sensation of feeling on top-of-the-world that made her grateful for every audition, go-see, and booking.

To be recruited in the female modeling realm is a game of chance. First, the girl must be genetically gifted of the highly demanding physical requirements. These requirements are so high that only three percent of the entire world fit the mold. A height of 5 feet 9 inches is considered short, and a hip width higher than thirty-four inches is considered *heavy*. From there ideal models can range from the classic girl-next-door, like a Victoria Secret model, to the unique bone structure of intense facial features, like the stunning Ruby Rose.

Daniellé Winters was already 5 feet and 7 inches by her sixth-grade year in school. At that height and age, most girls are drafted for either the basketball team or a modeling agency. With her intense bone structure, she was recruited by both. Originally, she thought modeling was very close to being and actor in the entertainment industry. After all, most of the celebrities she could name off-hand started out as models or actively worked in both fashion and entertainment.

That was alluring to her, but she was strongly encouraged to pursue basketball by her parents- because becoming a model is a startup business investment with the model being the product and service. So, she shied away from her soon to be destiny, but it wasn't long until she was astonished by the beauty the photos provided.

Daniellé's first modeling booking cast her as a woodland fairy with gold-leaf. She was skittish of the bright lights and the clicking of the photographer's fast camera shutter. She tugged at the rippled earthy green dress, and her red hair blew in every direction the fans aimed except for the few strands needed to get a decent shot. Daniellé felt like she was a puppet trying to balance upon a chair horizontally without falling. The art director, photographer, photographer's assistant, and client all held her by these imaginary strings. All in all, Daniellé was terrified and wanted to hide.

People around her gave directions on posing by announcing, "Chin up! Soft Hands! Think Whimsical!"

By the end of the photoshoot she was vomiting in the powder room from stress. In her mind there was absolutely no way anything productive could come from the last couple of hours and her modeling career was over before it even began. After polite salutations, Daniellé went home feeling defeated. A couple of weeks passed until the photographer's image retoucher returned with the edited print results.

Stung like a bee, but flying like a monarch butterfly, Daniellé's eyes 'stared jaw-dropped' at the photos.

On the digital reference image before her was a whimsical fairy looking like a cross between Lord of the Rings and Neopets. Her hair swept across the air. Her skin was resurfaced so that it had a pure cool almond tone, and her eyes shone bright like the works of the grand Peter Hurley.

That was the first chapter in a young inspired girl's life.

The next step was her first fashion runway show in city closest to her small hometown. With the introduction of live performance, high intensity, majestic designers, and the pulse-pounding action of the catwalk down the runway, Daniellé fell in love with the fashion industry. More photoshoots, runways, magazines, and commercials provided her with a feeling of being beautiful, a closest of unique brand-new clothing, travel, and income. As her career grew, she signed with another agency in Miami, Florida, and by the time she reached college it was helping cover tuition and living costs. It was work, but also a picture-perfect dream.

Daniellé's ambition and go-getter attitude longed that next tier of success. Which meant that if she was not going to be hopping the pond to London, Paris, or Milano, she needed to move to New York City to further her career. She wanted to sign with one of the Big Six modeling international agencies: IMG, Elite, Ford, DNA, Marilyn, or Wilhelmina. She wanted to grace the cover of Vogue or Wanderlust magazine. She wanted to strut the runways of Stella McCartney, Alexander McQueen, Marc Jacobs, and all her favorite designers. But that was not going to happen without an extra push. When a referral came in to apply to a modeling management team for fresh New York City faces that provided housing and business support, Daniellé applied right away. Months would pass, but in the spring of her

Junior year of college, Daniellé's world would change. An acceptance letter and a contract gave birth the happiest smile ever composed by the hopeful artist.

This was her ticket. This was her opportunity. This was her shot.

She felt like the flower girl, Girl Scout, prom queen, and beautiful bride all at once. Cloud nine was an understatement. She was going to be the next Coco Rocha, Kate Moss, or Cindy Crawford -even though she looked more the doppelganger of Cara Delevinge. She packed a bag and obtained means of airfare because it was time for Daniellé Winters and the Big Apple to meet.

Section One: Glamour

Glamour is all about the razzle dazzle. The attorney instructed Roxy to razzle dazzle in the incredible Chicago musical. The City of Dreams, The Big Apple, also best known as New York City, paired with the splendorous nature of the fashion world, is sure to place more than sequins in a young aspiring top model's eye.

A management group supported housing, and a chance at a ticket to success is all twenty-year old Daniellé could have imagined. She was going to achieve much beyond her small-town home limits. She was going to be a New York's next supermodel.

Just Around the Bend

Daniellé Winters was not much of a morning person until her second cup of white mocha flavored coffee, but the importance of today was an exception to her normal crankiness and a.m. drowsiness. With the sky still black with dawn approaching in an hour, she felt like her North Carolina home was a thousand miles behind her. Daniellé watched the city road's illumination reflectors and flickering of the freeway's street lights. Twirling her hair in excitement and nerves, she had barely touched the coffee in the cupholder. She had all the energy in the world for the upcoming events of the day. Her concern was more about traveling into the unknown land of New York City, completely on her own.

"Normally, a couple hours from now I would be waking up for work or school, but not today. Today marks the first day of the rest of my life! Today, I move to New York City for good! You hear me! These words do not even sound real. I feel like I am reading a bad script, but damn, what a script to read." Daniellé announced a monologue of cheesy excitement primarily to herself even though her roommate next to her was driving her to the airport.

Daniellé assured her success again with gestures as a powerful woman to her pocket mirror while applying her favorite Jeffrey Star red lipstick. Daryl Mandingae, her roommate/friend with benefits/possible boyfriend, was driving her to the airport before heading to work at the bakery. He baked in a mom-and-pop type shop just outside the city limits. Daryl stood around 6 feet 5 inches tall with rich chocolate toned skin and eyes. He spent most of his time dancing hip hop or writing. It was those commonalities that sparked a quick friendship between these practicing artists. Daniellé and Daryl were never good at defining their friendship, so it was often a confusing, yet amusing topic when they held get-togethers at their shared a home. For Daniellé, it was more about focusing on her career and schoolwork, and not getting too involved with anyone. For Daryl, it was about being all or nothing and family values. None of that would matter anymore though, as Daryl drove the redhead aspiring artist to have a chance to reach her dreams. All that mattered in this moment was keeping his eyes on the road instead of chuckling at Daniellé's pouty lips facial gesture to her mirror.

"You know, you are fine without all that demonic red paint on your face," he said with a hearty laugh.

Daniellé looked up to see if Daryl was admiring her or teasing her. She was never one hundred percent sure which was the case.

"Wearing Jeffree Star's lip sensation is not about being pretty, Daryl. It is about encompassing your inner potential and channeling that power to be transferred into productive energy. It is a statement that you are ready to take on anything life throws at you. In my case, life is bringing me N.Y.C and a *hell* of a shot to be a model, maybe even be an actress."

Daryl's chuckle transformed into a bountiful laugh. Now, he was teasing her.

"You are crazy, lady." He said as he barely held onto his composure.

He had talked with Daniellé several times about her dreams and goals in the fashion and acting departments. It had been her top priority since late childhood. He would playfully mock her if he saw her telling stories to a new friend of how she became interested in the industry by saying the rehearsed words with her. It was embarrassing to Daniellé, and nine out of ten times led to an annoyed glare. The other ten percent she may crack a smile.

Most people thought the small-town, North Carolina ugly duckling Daniellé would grow out of that nonsense of high fashion through her teens. Yet, her teenage years were good to her as she blossomed. Her jaw bone developed into a defined structure. Her neck was long with a delicate factor to it. She grew to 5 feet 9 inches tall in what seemed like overnight, and her symmetrical features added up in acceptable modeling requirement terms. She was lucky that her dream agreed with her genetic tools. It gave her a chance, so the dream blossomed right along with puberty.

Daryl was driving the girl to the airport wishing her the absolute best in what she was searching to achieve. He hid any sight of sadness about the decision to ask her to stay. He had attempted the conversation in a car ride last week, but one scared look from Daniellé halted it. Daniellé knew it was not easy on him, and it was not easy on her. She needed to leave though, and she was really hoping that Daryl would not ask her to stay. Since Daniellé's announcement that she'd signed with GAL management agency, she could hear him tossing and turning in his king-sized bed. Guilt-ridden she moved her bed in her room to the other side. After the announcement the whole house felt a little colder.

Daryl was not the only person or project she was giving up for the starlight vision. Daniellé was in the top three percent in the Health and Education class at her university. Starting at nineteen she had created and operated numerous businesses. She volunteered at Karm's and Fish Pantries without listing it on her resume, but she prayed every night before bed for this one shot.

She was not sure if Daryl could hear her prayers at night for a shot at her dreams. She tried to ignore the thought of it as she also attempted to genuinely pray for her enemies and, like every other female on the planet, to find true love.

Right before saying amen, she always repeated her promise to her future husband. "And for you. I pray God always gives your pain and tears to me instead. So, you never have a sad day in your life. I pray you never give up on finding me because I will never give up on finding you."

Love was the only tool powerful enough to make Daniellé to give up on the long shot dream, and with this knowledge she was always sure to protect herself from getting too attached to anyone. To her Daryl's silence meant he did not share his longing for more than casual fun. He was letting her go to live the dream instead of stranded in this town, and that was just the way life was going to be.

The song, *I Hope You Dance* played on the radio. It was an all-time favorite of Daniellé's. Her mother sang it to her as a lullaby growing up. She never fessed up to Daryl why she loved it so much, but occasionally he would find her dancing to the song while cleaning the kitchen on late weekday nights.

"Oh, please turn it up." she begged knowing that Daryl would cringe at the thought.

"Ugh…Okay." Daryl said while shaking his head in disappointment, "But then we listen to some real music."

A few minutes later Daryl's vehicle pulled up to the passenger loading dock. Absolutely no one was in sight, so he felt comfortable parking without the risk of being towed or ticketed.

"There you go, Vanessa. Take a short break," Daryl spoke to his SUV.

"That must be one of the weirdest things you do," Daniellé laughed as she joked.

"Weirdest? Coming from the woman that likes potato chips in her cookie dough and mint chocolate chip ice cream?" Daryl bantered back.

Looking down in slight embarrassment, Daniellé smiled at the thought of her guilty pleasure. She was going to need to give up ice cream and potato chips for an indefinite amount of time if she wanted to make the sizing needs. Daryl pulled Daniellé's suitcase from the trunk of the car.

"So, this is it?" he asked masking signs of ominous attitude.

Facing the long airport glass walls exhaling a long breath, Daniellé replied. "Yep, this is it."

She turned to find Daryl's face less than thrilled.

She quickly countered, "Not the end of this silly. I am still me. You are still you. And if everything goes as it should…," Daniellé lifted Daryl's head to see her eyes, "If everything goes as I want it to, it will all work out, and just be a page in our history. Ya know?"

Daryl produced a false smile. Daniellé even figured her own words were not likely, but she wanted to stay hopeful to the idea of *getting it all*. She knew that was selfish, and the guilt grew by the minute.

"Well, that is all one of them. You packed very light for moving," He started lifting Daniellé's suitcase as he leaned in for a hug. "Be safe, butterfly. I do not want to be going up there to save your punk ass."

"You know me! Stay safe or die trying to succeed. Either way, it works out." Daniellé laughed leaving him with a kiss on the cheek before turning to walk toward the American Airlines check-in.

"My first flight is just a connection. You see, I do not visit Tennessee much. The same type of culture but different mountain view, right? New York City will be so different though. My friend Landon found me an inexpensive standby ticket. He is a pilot. Don't you just love friend's like that?" Daniellé rambled on and on to the displeasure of a less than thrilled check-in clerk.

Most likely he was on the last leg of his shift, and Daniellé was making it as difficult as possible for it to be quiet and peaceful.

She did not notice her own annoyance as she kept talking, "Grass in the form of sidewalks, and trees in the form of skyscrapers are how I am envisioning New York City."

"Here are your documents. You may proceed to security," The counter man said dryly as he pointed toward security.

His mood temporarily dampened Daniellé's ecstasy-like spirits. She began thinking of how life's troubles are never as easy as stepping on a plane and leaving for a thousand-mile journey away from home. Her mind continued racing. No, God and the universe tend to have other plans and curveballs-like grumpy people in airports. Looking up at gate six, she realized the clerk's tone was highly appropriate.

"Seriously?! What are the chances?" Daniellé's mouth went dry as she dropped her handbag and suitcase to the floor.

God decided to force Daniellé to endure her greatest fear right before going aboard the connection flight.

Everyone has a person from their past that when their name crosses their mind, their blood begins to boil. For some it could be their mother-in-law, others the betraying ex-best friend, perhaps the bully from high school, and for Daniellé, it was Adam Maleficum. Adam was her first true, rawest, head-over-heels, boyfriend. Therefore, Adam was also her first true, rawest, head-over-heels, heartbreak. This boy, and yes boy despite chronological age being five years older than Daniellé and who was probably around thirty now, created the first scar in the relationship department. With his jet-black hair and crystal-bright eyes, Adam was now standing right in front of her with his hand held out for a handshake with the illusion that he would be giving her a warm embrace.

Daniellé thought deeply with her concern and anger. *If I was an outsider considering the situation, it could be amusing. But here I stand, a girl with a tied up messy bun, no makeup, and this charming and beautiful man was strutting right up to her with a perfect smile. Some women might even be jealous at this sight. I am going to be sick.*

Adam was the classic bad boy. The one parents warn their daughters about when in they're in high school. The older, older guy who wins the young girl over by breaking all the rules. Yet somehow, she was blinded to the fact that he had nothing good going for him, not even a decent, stable future. Daniellé had remained haunted by the stupidity that compelled her to keep forgiving this guy that had been in and out of jail during their entire relationship.

Daniellé's green eyes intensified as her body strengthened like a black cat wanting to pounce at Halloween. Adam's hand remained reached out as her mind played back the memories of her teenage years. The manipulation, the various types of abuse, all the creative lies, the pawning of her jewelry to get him out of jail, the conning his way out of any unfavorable light. Not to mention, that he had no business dating a girl five or more years younger than him. As if all of that was not enough to ruin a girl's version of Disney's true love, Adam cheated on her with *at least* three women she knew about. One of the mislead women on the list was only a year older than her. The gossip had gotten back to Daniellé's ears through the high school halls that Adam had accidently got her pregnant.

As sad as the situation was, the other girl's childbirth was most likely one of the best miracles for Daniellé's future. Daniellé could only pray the child would be a blessing to her unwanted list mate. It was the defining point of Daniellé and Adam's story. His actions would turn her blinders off to ignoring the madness of the situation, let her walk away, and be set her free.

Daniellé's mind came back to reality as Adam's eyes grew in shock at her rejection of his handshake. Her hand did too, but clearly for opposite reasons. Daniellé didn't know what her petrified mind was doing, as it went into autopilot.

"Hey Daniellé!" His voice was way too exuberant, especially for 5:00 a.m. "I haven't seen you in years. Where are you headed? I heard you were a big shot model now."

Daniellé's thoughts were as dry as an Arizona desert water faucet in the middle of August.

Of course. She thought. *Of course, this is happening.*

The population of their hometown, Perry, was only around thousand and questionably dropping, and big, or rather any, news travels fast in a small town.

The reminder that Adam only moved to her hometown those years ago to escape a warrant, replayed in her head as she let out a scoff.

How stupid can this guy truly be? Standing in front of me with all smiles. Daniellé wondered.

Her mind and body clearly on different pages the conversation, went forward.

Autopilot must have still been turned on as she answered, "Yes, traveling."

Her voice was strangely, yet confidently, dry and monotoned. He did not seem to get the hint because when she gathered her bags to find a distant seat, he sat next to her.

"I see you still journal. That's nice," He jokingly said.

At this point, she was no longer terrified. Daniellé was annoyed and borderline enraged. She was not the little girl anymore. She was an independent, strong-willed woman who was chasing her dreams full force.

Daniellé took a few deep breaths. She could easily have a panic attack.

God is testing my strength, giving me one last battle before New York City becomes home. She thought to herself.

"You say something?" Adam asked.

Right then, the terminal attendant called her name. "Daniellé Winters, please approach the terminal desk for flight number 101. Daniellé Winters."

Saved by the standby ticket from her pilot friend. Daniellé stood and walked slowly to the counter, and the attendant checked her ID. She made sure not to look like she was running away too fast.

The attendant informed Daniellé that she could go ahead and board the plane if she wanted. She thought it strange, but maybe the lady had noticed her interactions with Adam. Thrilled, she turned for a moment, and she saw Adam watch and awaiting her return pretending to be nonchalant. Picking up her items she stared at the floor instead of at him as she boarded.

She kept thinking I wish I would have said, "Don't come near me or my family...or frankly anyone I know, or even think of me again".

Daniellé cut off her anger prematurely. He just was not worth the time and energy.

She took her seat and buckled herself in for the ride.

I'm a better person than that. She thought. *I want to be a better person than that.*

Looking down at her arms though, the scars he's given her reminded her of the origin of hate. The first love is exactly that if it goes up in fire, the origin of hate. It burns intensely, destroying everything in its path, and leaves nothing but the undesired and staining ashes. Once upon a time it was new, and no one really knows what to expect of it…except *everyone* gets blackened by it.

Is it normal to get daily good morning texts and flowers, like aster and baby's breath, on special occasions or even just to say, 'I love you'? Do guys open car doors for their dates? Probably not. Daniellé laughed out loud at her thoughts. *Fairy tales. Lying grandmothers claiming they grant wishes.*

In her late middle teenage years Daniellé fell head-over-heels for an older man, mysterious bad boy type. She thought the burns and bruises on her back were because she was not a good enough girlfriend. She thought if she could just be better, it would go away, and they would live happily ever after.

It did not help that high school bullies had interpreted the marks on her body from rough sex. For that, she both thanked her lucky stars for the mistress girl who conceived and the high school bullies. She even prayed for them. Back then, Daniellé was simply young and stupid. A girl trying to find love in all the wrong places.

Models Stop Traffic • 20

The window seat would be just perfect for the upcoming sunrise, and Daniellé could think of a game plan to deal with Adam if he tried to approach her again. As her head leaned back in the uncomfortable headrest, she remembered how tired she would typically be this time of morning. Sleep was not an option for several reasons, so her thoughts decided to flow freely instead.

It all begins today. She recited over and over defining the underlying meaning of the words.

Adam took his seat in the front of the plane in 2A. He asked the flight attendant about switching, but Daniellé could hear the polite rejection telling him how it was against company policy. For once, Daniellé loved restrictions of policies.

For the next twenty or so minutes she started preparing for what could be a very hostile conversation when the plane landed. She came up with a million things she wanted to say, but at the same time, didn't have anything to say to him. She just wanted it to be over.

Yet, she wanted to tell him how wrong he had treated her. Not the fact that he pursued another girl, or rather girls, but how he could think it was okay in his dark, sick mind to cheat in addition to everything else. Daniellé was on the edge of seventeen with an unscarred heart. She was a virgin - pure and untouched. Then she experienced all of Adam's lies, drugs, cheating, and not to mention the times he left her stranded and abandoned in random places. He convinced her he was the only one who cared about her in the world. That she was worthless without him. The conditioning created an unremovable loneliness in her heart, a strong sense of never being good enough, and a fear of abandonment by the one she loved most.

Adam slowly over the course of inconsistent months had handcrafted scars on every cornerstone of the young girl's heart. He'd repeatedly ripped at it until he decided he wanted to take the whole heart for his collection. Daniellé had spent endless nights crying herself to sleep. Time was not going to let her forget how much power men possessed. They had the ability to destroy a woman from the inside out, to make her lose her mind in a maze of puzzles, and the ability to shatter a heart so much that the pieces could not even be found to attempt a repair. She had to be reborn and made anew to survive with a thick barrier of walls around the remaining shattered pieces.

So here and now on her way to New York City, Daniellé decided to let it go and not address Adam for her own health and emotional well-being.

An inspirational speech narrated in her head. She was no longer the small town southern belle of Perry. She was going to make it in her brand new shiny world and accomplish all her big city modeling dreams. She would pluck the daily thoughts of "I am not good enough" out of her mind.

The thought of Daryl's similar pep talks that morning played in her head. Those long meaningful conversations about life never ceases to amaze her. It was so easy to talk to Daryl. Sure, he could be judgmental, but he understood the struggling path of growth.

He was always saying, "I am a boy trying to be a man."

Daniellé's sarcastic response would be, "When will that day be here?"

Laughing like a roar he would respond, "When I die, baby-cakes."

Little did he know, she already knew he was a great man. With this thought she pulled out her journal again to write about the irony of her current situation.

Daniellé waited until the other passengers left the plane before she decided to stand up and gather her bags to leave. She wanted to give Adam plenty of time to move to wherever he was going before exiting the plane. She was not necessarily avoiding him as much as she just wanted to prevent conflict. Okay, yes, she was avoiding him- completely just avoiding.

The flight attendant thanked her for flying with them, and Daniellé smiled at her. As she left the plane Taylor Swift's *Welcome to New York* played on her pink iPhone 5C. She knew it sounded cheesy, but she found it very fitting to the scenario. So many times, she sang and danced in her old mirrored room to this song, never realizing that it could be entirely true one day. Daniellé felt some strong parallels with Taylor Swift, and in some regard perhaps that made her a Swifty. It just seemed Swift's lyrics just clicked for her.

Just as the chorus began to ignite a rock out session in the airport halls, Daniellé saw Adam waiting at the end of what was her personal runway. Suddenly, the shuffle feature changed the music choice to, *White Horse*. His eyes looked entirely too eager, and that paralyzing fear of her teenage years crept up. It was like one of those old time black and white movies where the python slither from behind the unknowing victim. It could easily bite her, but her intuition produced protection.

Daniellé's thought process attempted to direct her. *I am just going to walk right by him like he doesn't exist. One step, two steps, easy enough, right?*

Wrong.

As she arrived at the end of the connecting walkway, she felt someone grab her wrist. An overwhelming fury came over her as the full force of her left hand formed a fist that would land its swing just below Adam's chin. She missed. His eyes filled with shock at the failed attempt, but this time Daniellé stood her ground and did not back down. The two of them captured a small group of inquisitive people's attention.

Daniellé's naturally soft tone changed into a hiss, "Don't you ever touch me again."

Adam's hand dropped her wrist, and he fell silent. Daniellé repositioned her purse and began walking to the most public place she could find. Baffled at what had just occurred, she found an airport Starbucks. She saw that there were three within the terminal distance but decided to take residence at one with an actual enclosed area. With trembling hands, her fingers grazed over her left hand and wrist.

She was not entirely sure what had come over her that had caused such a drastic change her character, yet she felt so much better to have finally faced her biggest fear. It was like years of fear, regret, and anger were all swept away in one swift uppercut to Adam's jaw-failed or not. To add to her new-found glee, a very attractive mid-thirty something businessman who witnessed the encounter bought her favorite Starbuck's drink, Java Chip Frappe with no whip cream and a hint of cinnamon. She flashed him a smile, but he was already walking away.

The kindness of strangers. Daniellé said to herself baffled.

It was nice when men did not expect anything more than a thank you and smile from her, and this time she was not even given the chance to show her gratitude. It was not until she reached back for her journal that she realized that the gentleman had been dressed in a captain's uniform. Daniellé pulled out her journal and a pen from the bag to begin writing again about Adam, the mysterious gentleman, and her pilot friend Landon Kents.

Her journal entries recorded how Landon and Daniellé had originally not seen eye to eye. They met via the popular social app Zinder. When the two of them had finally physically meet up, it ended up in a most heated and pointless debate. For about an hour Landon and Daniellé went back and forth about southern and northern cultural stereotype differences. He had it drilled into his head that Daniellé was a classic southern woman, and he did not get along with southern people in general.

It was absurd, and even now Daniellé felt a little heated writing about the memory, but Landon and she decided friendship would be the best fit. Either way, she believed Landon was a decent guy. He did provide the $78.00 buddy pass ticket to New York City without her even asking. She could not have beat that price unless she was a pilot herself, and let us face it, Daniellé's dreams had a high cost.

Despite the rough start, Daniellé was grateful for Landon. As she wrote more in depth, the realization of her whole network of talented and career-minded friends was fundamental. Therefore, her first award acceptance speech should probably include the very long list of names for those who had helped her along the way. Among such names would be Landon Kents and maybe even the mystery man in uniform for a delicious drink at a stressful time.

Daniellé's journal entry changed quickly, like most of the thoughts in her ADHD mind.

She switched to a description of the highly technologically-advanced airport. Unlike any airport she had visited before, there were watchable tablets at the wine bars. The place just breathed a larger intensity and orderliness. She was disappointed she was unable to see The Statue of Liberty while flying, and even more disappointed to hear that it was only 55 degrees Fahrenheit outside.

At least allergies would be reduced at the cost of freezing temperatures! So, much for wearing my cut off shorts! She thought as she closed her journal.

It was time to take on the new adventure, and quite literally turn the page. But before Daniellé was to meet the GAL agency management team at the address for the Brooklyn model house, she was going to need a major anti-airport makeover. First, she would obtain her suitcase from the checked baggage terminal. Then she could try to pull off this dramatic switch from hillbilly to downtown Manhattan fashionista.

She nervously laughed as she talked herself through the process, "I do not know if this makes me less classy, but I need to head to the restroom to fix my hair, wardrobe, and makeup."

As Daniellé picked up her luggage from the belt terminal, she was shocked to learn from a Vietnamese accented lady that ID was required to receive her own luggage. For a moment Daniellé even wondered if it was one of those big city scams she had seen in movies.

But, no scam here.

In this New York City airport before you can pick up baggage, you must prove your identity with an approved ID.

Dorothy, we must not be in Perry anymore. Daniellé thought.

Daniellé spent almost forty-five minutes freshening up in the largest airport restroom she had ever seen, and then an hour, scared to death before she called for a taxi. Daniellé's nerves were going haywire as she dialed the digits.

Of course, a torrent of Daniellé's freaking out thoughts soon followed. *What am I going to see when I walked out those doors? What if the taxi driver takes me to the wrong address or tries to overcharge me? Will I look too much like I am a tourist? What if I get to the house, and this entire thing was some sort of joke?*

Daniellé's stomach churned as she grabbed her worry-filled head. She understood her overreacting, and she wanted to get a grip on her racing thoughts. Perhaps, the city-struck girl was just too overwhelmed. After all, she had been on planes the entire day, with the only source of food she'd had was a Starbucks frappe. But then again, she should be thankful for not eating. If she had eaten anything, she probably would have thrown up right now.

Daniellé collected herself as she pulled up the introduction email from Caleb Thornheart on her iPhone.

"This should calm me down some," She said to herself.

Daniellé read the model introductory email.

"Hello, Ladies!

GAL agency officially launches in less than 12 hours for new models of the house!

We have exciting plans already in place for you between your photo shoots, castings, go-sees, fashion shows, etc. Remember that you now live in the Concrete Jungle! And it is true that everyone is here for the hustle. So, do not expect it to be easy, and be careful who you trust!"

Daniellé thought this was one of the strangest and least assuring introductions emails she had received to date, but perhaps New Yorkers welcome newbies with disclaimers and warnings instead of a southern saying like, "Glad to meet y'all! "

After the introduction, the girl's names were listed, along with their room numbers. Space was going to be tight with only two small bedrooms with bunk beds piled up to the ceiling on both sides. Yes, Daniellé was going from a spacy three-bedroom home with Daryl to estrogen Mount Everest.

That was going to be interesting, but she hoped there would be some type of local coffee shop to stay at when not working.

She looked in the email receipt section to see the names of the women she would be calling roomies. Daniellé knew it was not a good comparison, but she imagined this would be like a sorority house. Of course, the roommate models were going to be beautiful, a certain amount of high maintenance, and on a mission -if they were anything like Daniellé. In the email the girl's names read: Daniellé, Savannah, Kathleen, Calista, Rana, Amy, Lauren, Imogen, Bebe, and the list just went on from there. She felt special that her name was listed first but tried to not read too much into it. She remembered when applying that there was a gender option available, but apparently no males made the cut.

So…many…roommates. Daniellé thought. *These girls are from all over, even different countries. How am I supposed to even talk with some of them?*

Nonetheless, Daniellé tried to familiarize herself with the list of estrogen as her cortisol levels increased slowly. When Daniellé finally flagged down her first taxi she attempted to put her acting skills to the test. She handed the thickly accented driver her bags, got in the backseat, and said the address like it was her mother's.

Daniellé must have performed well as the driver replied. "What is it like to be home?"

She smiled and sentimentally said, "Home, yes. I have been waiting some time to be here."

As he drove Daniellé toward Brooklyn, her eyes filled with amazement as she crossed the famous bridge.

Escaping one last time from her lips, Daniellé whispered, "Yes. I'm home."

We've Only Just Begun

The taxi fare was fair as he charged her the appropriate amount for the trip, and the hustle and bustle of the model house was already in full bloom as Daniellé arrived through the front door. She could hear a voice in the back unpacking as she searched for the spot she would claim as her own.

"There. Perfect. Now stay," Bebe spoke to the Go-pro camera in high pitched valley girl fashion.

She was in a full-on testimonial story with her camera. It was becoming apparent that she would need the stability feature during the editing phase. After several attempts, she positioned herself in one-quarter frame for her selfie filming. She began a discussion with her soon-to-be YouTube audience.

"Ever play hot lava growing up? It's the game where players jump couch to couch with brooms trying to not fall to their doom, a.k.a., the softly carpeted living room. The model house was a lot like that. There was a total of three bedrooms with two itty bitty bathrooms. Each of the rooms was the size of about three Harley Davidson's parked next to one another, and the girls are packed in like sardines in bunk beds stacked up to the top of the walls. All of them, except for like two girls, broke the one suitcase rule, so these sardines had tin cans piled up to the ceilings as well.

"So much for thinking no one else would break the rules." Bebe spoke in the direction of the camera.

She did not even realize Daniellé, newly arrived, stood outside the small room unintentionally listening to Bebe's one-person video conversation. Daniellé was confused about her room placement. Her name did not seem to be listed on either door. So, she was making herself at home in the hallway for now-with her one suitcase.

Bebe knew she was easily annoyed, so she decided to have the lower bunk next to the air conditioner. It was the maximum distance she could arrange away from her roommates in the limited space. If she reached out an arm she was guaranteed to hit the next person's bunk or the actual model.

"The girls are all gorgeous here -at least according to their social media photos. It's almost like no one is gorgeous as a result," she explained to her camera audience.

After fiddling with the blanket covers for a few minutes, Bebe forgot her camera was still set to record. She nestled up in her Bob Marley blanket and shuffled through her books about holistic medicine practices. It was not until the girl above her slammed her suitcase -no not suitcase, suitcases onto the bed above her -that Bebe realized she had still been filming for the last several minutes. Never one to pass up a potential opportunity, Bebe thought this would be a great moment to capture on film. She faced the camera upwards to see her new top-bunk mate's appearance.

As she peered up from the bottom bunk, Bebe saw a girl who looked like she was straight out of Hollywood. Wearing a red and tan cheetah styled fedora, big white sunglasses, and a Peace. Love. And Surf. half-tee, the beach blonde beauty was speaking loudly to someone on the phone.

"Really ma, it will be fine. I get along great with everyone. No worries." The Hollywood chick said in an L.A tone.

Impressed by beauty but not by words, Bebe rolled her eyes and tucked her head back under the bed. Obviously, she went unnoticed by the beach babe, and she was not exactly convinced everyone got along with the type of people who slam suitcases on beds without noticing those around her. Both girls may have been displaying some sense of entitlement.

The beach blonde went on talking for nearly twenty minutes before she realized Bebe was under her bunk. By this point, Bebe had plugged her ears with headphones to ignore the blonde's rambling about finding the nearest beach over at Coney Island. Daniellé from the hallway just giggled at the phone conversation she heard over the undertone of loudly played earbud music.

The beach blonde looked under the bed and said genuinely surprised, "When did you sneak by?"

Bebe removed her headphones, and replied, "Twenty minutes before you arrived. Maybe even thirty."

Daniellé smiled at the snarky remark from outside of the room. To her this seemed like the beginning of a former top model Tyra Bank's television drama.

The blonde looked puzzled but brushed off the reply as potentially rude. Instead she ignored the comment completely and said her goodbyes on the phone. She began unpacking her items onto the bed while humming loudly.

Daniellé was shocked the beach blonde's parents might have driven her to the airport. It was so different from to her experience. Her mother and father wished her some version of the worst of luck and told her to start thinking about college instead of the fashion industry. Daniellé was just ignored when she talked about her dreams and her move to N.Y.C. It was very similar to the way the beach blonde walked by her in the hallway a few minutes ago without noticing the red head sitting in the middle of it.

The Hollywood blonde began decorating her top bunk wall with photos of her boyfriend and the beach. A large canvas of Polaroids was precisely decorated in a scattered layout with wooden single letters spelling out S.V.G. above the photos. Bebe's annoyance grew as she noticed a few of the G-photos had tumbled down next to her bunk. She handed them back to her new roomie through the crack without a word. When the beach blonde remained oblivious Bebe addressed her more directly.

"Hey, unless you want to be S.V.C, you will need these back," Bebe said in sarcastic tone.

"Oh, thanks. And it is Savannah Vanessa Giles. Raddest name ever, right?" S.V.G commented matching Bebe's sarcasm with her own tang of snippiness.

Bebe laughed heartily at her quick reply while picking up more fallen photos, "It is definitely grabbing my attention."

She respected the snippy tone in Savannah's answer, but the respect only lasted for a moment. Bebe felt slighted when she saw that her joke had gone completely over Savannah's head, but Daniellé was laughing from the hallway. Bebe and Savannah both swung a look toward the door confused. Bebe quickly realized she was never going to be able to concentrate on her camera or book, so she attempted to nap to some bohemian music.

Still waiting for guidance from the management team or really anyone, Daniellé turned her focus away from Bebe and Savannah to compose a message to her best friend Angelia, back home.

Daniellé started out the message in all caps stating, "THIS IS OVERWHELMING!!!"

She continued to describe how cramped the apartment was for people living in it. The closest comparison she could to provide Angelia was from a shared memory of theatre summer camp back in grade school. Angelia and Daniellé had shared a small tent with five other thespians that summer. By August it was a miracle any of them were still walking the planet.

After the description, she told Angelia that some of the models were to set to arrive later that night, but she could not find anyone to tell her the correct room assignment for herself. Daniellé's main concern was that she would lose her chance to have a top bunk. If this confusion persisted she considered claiming a top bunk in both rooms long enough for her to figure out which one would be her new fraction of personal space in the model house. Her last comments were about how the others broke the one suitcase rule, and her certainty that she was not going to enjoy these living arrangements. She hit send and tucked her electronic device into her handbag.

Daniellé had no sisters, and most of her friends were male except for a couple of college friends and Angelia. She recalled from her friend's stories and television shows how sisters bicker over the smallest of subjects and steal each other's clothes. As a result, she wondered if she would need to hide her personal items from the others with these tight, jail-like conditions.

After she came out of her trance, Daniellé smiled as two, staring puzzled girls walked by her. She had been clearly labeled as the weirdo in the hallway staring off into space.

When Bebe looked up, she now felt like the oblivious one. Another two models had arrived since she shut her eyes. Bebe saw the embroidery that said "Imogen" on the side of one the extremely pale girl's suitcases. Its owner looked pure as snow from head to toe.

The name "Amy" was written in pink cursive on a handbag for the other new roommate. Bebe thought it was strange how much her each of these girls liked their names on things –the wall, suitcases, purses. She did not have a single item in her current or past that ever had a monogram on them.

"Hey, team meeting," an unknown deep female voice, later identified as Lauren's, shouted from the doorway.

Bebe pulled on her shawl and untangled her GoPro string from the bed. She followed the herd to the living room. It took only one quick catty corner turn to reach the 'shared living space'. One large couch and a flat screen TV lined one wall, but a total of more than twenty bodies packed themselves into the tiny space. Most of the girls sat or kneeled on the floor, while the ones who managed to find couch space spread their long legs out, leaving no room for others. Bebe found a seat on the floor in one of the corners, while Amy squished her way into the small empty slot on the couch. They made a small space and tried to encourage the brightly red-headed girl to sit with them. Instead, Daniellé smiled at their gesture and stayed seated on the floor with Bebe. Daniellé had not spoken directly to

Bebe yet, but the conversation she overheard between Savannah gave Daniellé the impression the two of them might get along.

"Maybe it is a good thing?" The fiery-flamed Daniellé mumbled to Bebe.

Bebe looked at Daniellé with a bewildered look on her face. She did not realize that Daniellé had been the one laughing at all her remarks earlier, nor did she understand the reference point of her current question.

In a peppy interruption, an Adriana Lima look-alike smiled at Bebe and Daniellé saying, "Hey, want a seat up here, or you?"

Daniellé looked up in awe at the girl for a moment, but she just replied with a smile and said, "No, thank you."

The girl brushed it off smiling as well and invited Bebe again to sit with her. Bebe jumped at the chance to be off the floor. Daniellé shrugged to herself looking around at the group. She found herself analyzing the wide assortment of models in the room.

With so many beauty queens in the room. Photoshop? Surgery? Daniellé thought.

The saying 'we're not in Kansas anymore' came to mind. A strong familiar voice roared over the small talk chatter. It clearly demanded attention.

"Welcome to New York, ladies." Caleb Thornheart, one of the directors of GAL agency, announced.

The models recognized the voice of the man who had completed their individual selection interviews. Caleb wore a blue pant suit and stood in the center of the room. Voices commented on the classic retro look from last year's C.C. fashion show in awe of his style.

Caleb's pounding voice roared across the chatter still. This second time around, everyone's attention was captured by the attention it demanded. Big boned, Caleb was not one to start a fight with, today or any other day. His head nearly touched the ceiling of their small townhouse.

Daniellé was scared for a moment until she realized she knew the voice from earlier phone calls. Caleb Thornheart was one of the interviewers on the director board she'd talked to before embarking on this adventure. Words echoed through her memory about the interview process, and his comments of Daniellé's washboard abs and flaming red hair. Fear turned into an eager smile with a rainbow effect happening across the room as each model came to the same realization.

Caleb began his introduction to New York City by starting with the current living arrangements.

"Each of the models all will have at least six to nine roommates in their room at any given time. So be focused on your mission and reason here instead of on one another. I also will be living here in my own personal room next to the kitchen. This room is completely off limits to anyone without my explicit permission. You all will share the one-bathroom and the one closet in each bedroom with your roommates. The kitchen is reserved for me unless otherwise stated. There may be some labeling of allowed cabinet drawers as food is prohibited in the bedroom areas. The apartment building does have a floor above us and below us, so be mindful of that as well. You all will be working non-stop, so do not be alarmed if new models arrive while others move on due to the lack of endurance in this hustle."

Everything Caleb said sounded well-rehearsed. He continued the introduction of other management members. He paced in the small area allowed, and it reminded Daniellé of a military sergeant.

"Richmond is our director of castings, and he will be arranging everything behind the scenes. Lastly, Leviathan is our director of finance for the management group. You all will not be seeing much of him unless we have special outings. There is one more director, but we will introduce him some other time."

After the introductions, the men stood up and walked out without giving any salutations. They looked as if they had been forced to be there. They might as well have been children being scorned to eat their green vegetables. The models looked around the room searching for their next directions. Caleb noticed the confused sea of faces and suggested the models get to know one another through a game, but he did not initiate anything before dismissing the meeting.

Call My Name

"Hey! Does anyone want to go to Smoothie King? It is only a half mile walk?" Lauren yelled across the house.

Lauren was the type that normally tried to keep away from anyone she could, but walking the streets of Brooklyn, New York alone sounded a little too dangerous for her taste. Much to her displeasure, the two girls she liked the least agreed to the walking trip, Rana and Daniellé.

It had been about a week and half since the introduction meeting in the model house. The models had received some papers of upcoming events including casting calls and extreme makeovers. Among the rest of the packet were notes on managing the grid of Manhattan, New York City. Lauren had always been the quick to judge type, and despite her tough looking exterior shell, she was as insecure as the others -if not more. She just did not know how to hold her composure. Thus, her insecurity caused a heightened strain between her and the other models. Each one of them had at least one attribute Lauren envied and the only way she could hide it was striking annoyed faces and gossiping to the others when given the opportunity. Her favorite targets were Daniellé and Calista. Perhaps, she was the most jealous of them, but the person her attitude hurt the most was her.

In all reality, Lauren had many physical qualities going for her. Her strong jaw created striking images with her blunt lob brunette hairstyle. Lauren was easily labeled as the top potential anhydrous model of the house. Along with that, she could eat for days without gaining weight in her waistline. That prevented her from ever feeling the need to starve herself like some of the others until Richmond mentioned her hips not fitting the designs for her portfolio shoot the following week. The comment offended her deeply, so Richmond was placed on her personal gossip hit-list from that moment on too.

Rana, feeling cheesy, nudged Daniellé from her top bunk. "Hey, I want a smoothie. It is bo-go! So, let's, you know, go."

Daniellé was really enjoying her new roomie's corny sense of humor. It was not hard to win Daniellé over when it came to free or cheap food, so she hopped down from her bed in agreement. Smoothies were becoming her main meal because of their low-caloric intake.

"You want to come too, Scarlett? Calista?" Daniellé said invitingly.

Scarlett had arrived a few days later than most of the other models in the house. In fact, the house residents had nearly doubled plus a half the past week. Caleb was not kidding about the turnover rate this place possessed.

Daniellé was a few years younger than Scarlett, but they clicked very well. From Chicago, Scarlett was shorter than all the others in the house standing at 5 feet 6 inches. Her raven hair draped down to her hips, and her eyes shone a bright sky blue.

Scarlett was the most educated about fashion designers in the home. It amazed Daniellé the extent of detailed information Scarlett had about designers like Stella McCartney and J. Crew, even though it annoyed the others. They thought it came off as snotty. It did not phase the raven beauty though. Except for Daniellé, Scarlett preferred to be left alone anyways. Daniellé respected the passion for learning the trade better, which it caused the instant click in their friendship.

The two of them spent their downtime educating Daniellé while on city girl date nights. At first it made Daniellé uncomfortable since she could not afford the dinner and outings she was being given by the well-off Scarlett. Daniellé soon realized that Scarlett was not affected by the Daniellé's financial needs, and she just wanted her roommate's company.

Daniellé's smoothie question was ignored as Scarlett was very focused on watching Gossip Girls on Netflix, and Calista was heavily into a nap.

Rana nudged Daniellé again referencing their inviter's outfit, "You know it is funny that she comes with her own leather jacket." Rana pointed to Lauren as the exited their room.

"We all come with our own leather jackets, jean jackets, and heels. We might as well be Barbie's with accessory kits." Daniellé laughed.

As they walked out of the townhouse, Daniellé started a conversation about the introductory meeting. The three models were happily surprised to see some new friendly faces outside in the patio area. Alice and Elise were a contracted film crew from the agency. The two of them were students at Columbia University, and their focus was on creating a documentary about modeling. They had very restricted access to the models at only specific times, but the girls of the house enjoyed the interviews.

Shutting the iron gate behind the three of them Rana asked, "What did you guys think of that meeting or of any of this so far?"

"That is a great question! It came out so naturally. Could you ask it again so, I can get it on tape?" Elise and Alice were ready for good footage with equipment in hand.

"Um...sure," Rana replied in dazed acceptance as Lauren rolled her eyes. Setting back up at the top of the stairs before closing the gate Rana asked again, "So, what did you all think of that meeting last week or of any of this so far?"

"Lame. It felt a lot like a school orientation," Lauren muttered.

Rana looked at the camera and began explaining, "I was expecting a lot different when I came here, too. So, many pageant queens, and it looked like one girl just came from one of those perfect teeth commercials. Was it Colorado Barbie or something? I can't remember her name now. But it is pretty cool overall."

Daniellé, Alice, and Elise giggled at the comment.

"Her name is Kathleen, but she does look like the perfect Barbie doll with that long platinum hair," Alice explained.

A half mile later, the girls found themselves under the subway station tracks walking into Smoothie King. The teenage employee at the front counter of the Smoothie King ignored them when they entered. It was an odd setup as Lauren and Daniellé were not used to having grocery shops also attached to restaurants and bars. It reminded them a lot of an airport setup. People were even sleeping in some of the table booths. The five of them took a seat in the booth across from the sleeping woman using her briefcase as a pillow.

"Is that normal?" Lauren asked puzzled.

Alice nodded yes, and she clicked back on the camera. She pointed at Daniellé to start talking to the camera.

"Okay. Well, we all introduced ourselves afterward. That was a bit awkward. Caleb said it would be a little bit crazy for a couple more days as more girls arrived. The initial plan was to keep to myself as much as possible and stay focused on booking gigs, but Rana and Scarlett are making that a little impossible." Daniellé explained with a teasing smile at her friends.

Lauren jumped into the conversation shifting the camera's focus, "I am mainly doing this because I did not feel like going to college yet, and my mother said I needed to do something with my gap year. I am hoping it can create some income for these empty pockets." She turned to the sign, and said, "Who wants to split the cost on the BOGO smoothies?"

Alice stood up with the camera to join Lauren at the counter and ask more questions.

Rana followed them saying, "I will just get us the same type Daniellé, and you pay me when I sit down. It is only $2.35 with the BOGO for each of us."

Daniellé asked Elise if she planned on getting a smoothie. Elise shook her head no.

"I just ate a little while ago. So, now that it is just us. What would you really like to say about the living arrangements or anything else coming up?" Elise asked with an eager look on her face.

Daniellé thought for a moment about the chaos of moving in over the last days. After a few moments, she looked back at Elise and started to answer.

"This place. This house, this city, these people…They are nothing like I thought. My goal is to really make something incredible happen in my life. I have a casting call each day next week, and I am already being tagged on Instagram as the "Girl on Fire." It is truly a unique experience to hear people call my name, well kind of, but I also know I have a lot of work to do here. I do not want to get caught up in the house drama or quite frankly anything that will deter me from my dreams. The Sara Zelly portfolio shoot is tomorrow. Hint, that's why I am very hesitant to eat anything today including that small smoothie coming my way. I just want this all to go perfectly, you know? I need a perfect book, a perfect casting week, and just a dash of the right amount of perfect luck." Daniellé's words came straight from the heart.

"So, here is to perfect, right?" Rana handed Daniellé her smoothie as the camera captured them both in the frame of Alice's lens.

Elise smiled realizing that these models were not just bobble heads but had a true passion like she did for her work.

Glam

Glamour. Fashion. Lights.

Style. Shoes. Runway. Fame.

Calista's whole body trembled despite Daniellé's hand holding her wrist steady. The beat of the music shook the floor and lights beamed in every direction. After only a little over four weeks in N.Y.C, the two of them had been booked, met design standards, and were now on the set of their first New York fashion show. The quick sunrise on their dreams left them a little too dazzled. Neither of them had attended runway training yet. They had honestly shocked the directors of GAL agency with such a quick booking without assistance.

"We can do this. This is what we practiced at home. So, pull yourself together." Daniellé directed releasing Calista's wrist.

The two of them had all but worn down the wooden floors of the model house. They practiced each day for a minimum of five hours. Their main goal was to not make fools of themselves.

The leadership and calm qualities of Daniellé's personality showed up in times of high-stress such as these. Calista felt her arms go limp as they fell to her sides, and her giraffe-like long legs were about to follow suit.

However, with a good all-over shake, Calista released her fear and self-doubt. She was meant to be here. Both had earned this booking.

Neither of them had walked for designers as well-known as Queen or Chao. Sure, they had walked in fashion shows in their hometowns, but this was New York City. The strut is completely different in New York compared to Los Angeles, Atlanta, and even Miami. It was more determined and serious in each step. Walks in Miami held pride and quickness. Yet Calista would walk the runway in an elegant silk halter dress, and Daniellé would strut down the runway in a designer dress coat suitable for a celebrity of Blake Lively's status. After all, the rich and famous were the target audience of events like these. No one middle or lower class could afford these clothes without getting into an enormous amount of credit card debt. But models didn't have to worry too much, since nine times out of ten the walking *clothes hangers*, a poor nickname for models, were not wearing the true fabrics, but less expensive versions. The designers were smart enough to know runway shows could lead to frayed hems, lost beading, and rips from pins.

When the astonishment of Calista and Daniellé's crazy reality tired them even for a moment, a blast of the New York fashion show aura would wake them back up. The intensity of the air carried the energy throughout the room- or was that just the high-powered fans?

Calista gasped for air, "There is truly nothing more glorious. Am I really even here?"

Daniellé jaw dropped looked up at the thirty-foot ceilings. Metal spheres hung from the rafters with metallic spikes shooting in each direction. The beaming strobe lights bounced light to each section of the stage. The runway itself was illuminated like teal seawater while the pure white curtains hide the backstage. The icing on the cake was a haze of fog that was released on a thirty-second timer that rose from under the stage. Calista and Daniellé would present the latest fashion with fifty other models in only a couple hours' time.

"I sure hope so, but if not, I can stay here anyways." Daniellé commented still looking out at her surroundings.

The backstage lighting and audio crew was testing everything for that night's performance, and several interns were setting up white folding chairs along the t-shaped catwalk stage. Workers like busy bees weaved between the two girls occasionally shooting annoyed looks at them as they stood there pondering. Some of the audience would be standing but a selected few had the privilege of front row seats.

"We must look like fresh meat standing here." Daniellé chuckled hinting at her embarrassment.

"I do not see how anyone could get used to this." Calista flashed her gap-toothed smile in reply.

Calista reached for Danielle's hand as she focused on where they were to check-in. For a moment Danielle stared at Calista's frail, recently moisturized, hand in hers. An emotion was there, but she did not know what to call it. It was like an autumn leaf tornado in the middle of an empty street at the flash before a pink and golden sunset. Everything was fleeting just as it started, but the beauty of the moment was enough to captivate Danielle. She was not sure how this story would go, but she would rather be still in this position for the rest of her life than risk breaking it with her clumsy movement. Her thoughts ended, yet clarity was not to be found.

"There it is. See the sign? Danielle?" Calista asked.

As she woke from her haze, Danielle followed the tug of her hand. Entering backstage through a small entry hallway curtain, the atmosphere changed from jaw-dropping to back-breaking. There were people packed in shoulder-to-shoulder dashing about on various missions, and racks of clothing lined the room. Designers walled off their sections with racks full of their latest designers and signs printed with their names and the names of the models who belonged in the station. Hair stylists and make-up artists swarmed the models in full three hundred and sixty-degree angles. Tugging, pulling, pushing, and jostling were the norms of a backstage runway. Most clothing pieces hanging from the racks were worth more than what Daniellé paid for her car back home even if they were not the true fabrics. The shoes alone were worth more than most new sets of tires.

"Hey. We are here to check-in. I am Calista. Last name is Ahmann. Number 32. And this is Daniellé Winters number 67 from the auditions, right?" Calista said to the table production assistant.

Calista looked at Daniellé for confirmation. Daniellé nodded back at the check-in attendant. Daniellé was still absorbing the dazzle of the environment, but she quickly remembered she needed to be professional.

The booth was the only simply designed item in the room, and even then, it was not too basic. It was a just pull-out table with black table cloth draped over it. It had a sign on the front said C.F.N.Y. Show in white Garamond font, and there were a few trinket souvenirs on the table. Yes, the check-in table was the subtlest of items in the room.

"Great. Here are your numbers, programs, a reminder of times, clothing numbers, backstage passes, and list of designers- not that you could ever forget who you are walking for...Oh, and here is a map of the stage, and wrist band for the food tables. Obviously, do not eat in the clothing. Do not even *breathe* on the clothing. Also, since you both are just walking for the one designer, if you wish you can go to the extra and fill-in room? We may be able to fit you in one of their empty slots. Okay. You are good to go." The attendant spoke uncannily fast.

Blank-faced Daniellé and Calista looked at their newly found resources with puzzled looks on their faces. The information was extensive, but perhaps this was the way to prevent any mishaps.

Which way was Chao from Queen, and what do you do for fill-ins? Daniellé worried silently.

The lightning fast introduction caught both Calista and Daniellé off-guard. The lack of sleep and food was most likely an extra contributor to their lack of focus. Daniellé craved a glass of water, but not even that was a smart idea. No model wants to look bloated on stage. Daniellé pulled out a site map. It appeared more like a shopping mall than backstage. She pointed out to Callista that the fill-in room was in the back side right corner.

Later, Daniellé would learn about a conversation talking about her from one of the models in the house, but right now, Calista and she were about to live out their dreams.

Meanwhile, back at the house, Scarlett, Rana, Amy, and a couple of other models lounged in the living area. Each of them stretched out as much as possible to mark the territory of the little space found in their house. As in most confined quarters, territory and clicks become second nature. Even invisible walls can give one a false promise of privacy. Now, they all began to slowly realize that privacy did not exist in this place- not by walls, secrets, or even when they thought they were alone. GAL agency failed to mention that they might always be watched somehow while in the house. It was a mysterious wonder how information was always brought to the surface even when someone hadn't told a soul. No one could find any proof one or one way or another if cameras or a rat was a possibility. One thing was certain though, nothing was personal information.

Even though the girls could agree management did not have privacy for the models, the girls of the houses were too caught up in their own drama to notice.

"You think Carrie would put some flats in her purse. Those shoes are expensive." Scarlett commented to the TV screen.

"Only you would really know how expensive." Rana said poking fun at Scarlett. In their bedroom sat Scarlett's collection of designer stilettos, pumps, cones, and kitten heels lining the walls.

"Don't be jelly, Rana. We can't all be shoe size 8 and Scarlett's favorite… Expensive shoes? … Nights in the city? … If you did not have a boyfriend in Chicago…" Amy commented.

"If Daniellé is Scarlett's favorite, why is Daniellé always trying to hide at the nearby coffee shop?" Rana asked. "Honestly, people are always at opposites when it comes to Daniellé -either love or hate."

Lauren and Kathleen crossed the living area with two shopping bags in each hand.

"Not mine. That girl seems like a total bitc-." Lauren was cut off by Kathleen's shocked gasp of innocence.

"You really do not cuss or do anything wrong, do you?" Amy asked Kathleen.

"I just don't think it is right to gossip. Especially when they are not even here." Kathleen said shyly to the others.

After an eye roll, Lauren plopped down on the floor next to Amy.

"That is exactly when you are supposed to speak the truth. That way they can't stop you." Lauren said.

"Sounds like the cowardly thing to do, but after all, you are the gossip queen. Oh, sorry. Dancing queen, right?" Rana said annoyed.

"Bite me." Lauren hissed while collecting her bags to stand again. She furiously walked back toward the bedrooms.

Refocusing the conversation, Kathleen asked, "Why do you think Daniellé and Calista did not tell us about the casting call they had? We could have tried out too."

"It is simple math. If they share it with us, and we're cast in the show, they're out of the job. I do not think they even told each other until they saw one another at the casting call." Scarlett explained. "Besides, I am not tall enough for runway, so I am not pissed except for the fact that I did not get to see the show."

"And why are we not there, exactly?" Rana said rushing to her feet. She darted to the back room to grab her shoes, a flip back hat, and her handbag.

"Well, are you all coming?" Rana asked from the back room.

Kathleen, Amy, and Scarlett took a moment to stare at each other. Scarlett and Kathleen joined Rana in collecting their things.

"Well, we should at least go somewhere to get out. Let me get my subway card to reload." Kathleen said.

"Forget the subway. Let's Uber." Scarlett suggested.

Birthdays

When someone is a model, age is NOT just a number. It's one more point against them in a game. A game in which the lower the number the better. It does not matter if it's age, waist, bust, hips, or even feet. The only desirable high number is height, and that is something dieting, yoga, and hours of cardio can't change.

When Daniellé felt like she experienced two birthday parties in one long hazy experience, it felt like she'd aged two years instead of one. This was the case here. Not all the events of her extended birthday happened together, but Daniellé's twenty-first birthday, like most twenty-first birthdays, was a beautiful blur of wonderful, crazy events over a course of some distorted amount of time. So, while all the events happened, who knows exactly how they unfolded the way they did.

Flipping back over the twin bunk beds purple comforter, Daniellé remembered immediately that today marked her twenty-first birthday. She let out a sigh as she hid under the blanket staring through the thin cloth straight to the ceiling. Anywhere else in the world freshly legal drinking aged girls would be heading to a party or at least to the kitchen's pantry, but Daniellé was heading straight back underneath the covers. Being older brought no joy to her mission. She felt like a failure for not being where she wished to be at this stage of her life by now. Sure, most people believe that at twenty-one you're still just being a wet-behind-the-ears child, but in the modeling world, you're practically a grandmother. Under the blanket, she felt safe from agencies, casting directors, and the whole industry's judgement.

Some of her roommates, however, had other plans as they turned on the lights and screamed, "Happy Birthday!"

Rana attempted to pull the covers from Daniellé's hands.

"Come on! It is a good thing. Be happy!" She insisted.

Daniellé was far from happy about today, but she knew her acting skills could keep her friends from noticing. She released her grip of the covers giving Rana full control of exposing her aged face to the universe. Along with the bright light shining in her eyes, Daniellé saw six pairs of gleamingly excited eyes. Rana was eagerly accompanied by Scarlett and Imogen.

Before Daniellé could sit up, Rana began singing a perfectly pitched happy birthday, while Imogen and Scarlett jumped around cheering, 'Another year older!' and 'Cha, Cha, Cha.' Scarlett hit the play button on her phone. Methodically planned out, Selena Gomez's voice mixed in with the birthday cheer.

A bit overwhelmed, Daniellé said, "You all are crazy." but mid-sentence, she was already smiling at the joyous aura in the room.

Amy opened the door to join the early morning party. Greeting everyone, she introduced an idea, "How about we head down to Times Square? The billboards and flashing lights are so incredible! I have been there three times in the last week!" She paused. "Don't judge me."

"Sounds like fun. What do you think birthday girl?" Rana asked as she danced around with Scarlett and Imogen.

"I do not know." Daniellé's voice said hesitantly.

Daniellé's mind was still focused on the damage aging could do to her career choice. She could feel the aura changing to sadness around her, but when her eyes met Imogen's, who looked like she was about to cry in disappointment, she caved.

Alright," Daniellé replied, still getting her head wrapped around the dance party in their room.

"Well, I have a gig today. So, I can't, but I will be partying with you all tonight!" Scarlett reminded the group.

"We also need to get you some 'Happy 21st Birthday' gear. I am thinking a tiara and pageant sash!" Amy insisted, as a past beauty pageant winner.

"I have never had one of those before." Daniellé envisioned herself looking like Miss America.

"Then get out of bed! Time's a wasting. You know it takes a while to get to the city!" Amy announced.

Everyone transitioned from dance party to hustling around getting ready.

As the girls piled into the small bathroom like a clown car, Caleb walked up holding a breakfast banana and coffee. One model was showering, two models were fixing their hair and makeup in the mirror, and one waited outside the doorway for a chance to get into the mix. It made for a hilarious image overall.

"What are you all up to?" Caleb drowsily asked.

Imogen rushed by him with curlers in her hair.

"It is Daniellé's birthday. We are going to Times Square," she replied.

"Oh yes, where is the birthday girl?" Caleb inquired. "I would like to join you all. We will have a light lunch together."

Daniellé was clearly one of Caleb's favorites, and sometimes it created resentment among the others. But the mention of free food brought cheer instead of jealousy.

Most of the girls were beginning to struggle heavily financially. Some of the crew still would have rather that Caleb not go for 'fun' sake, but it was not like they could have said no to their manager anyways.

"I'm in here!" Daniellé shouted from the shower. "They let me have first shower dibs."

"Great! Well, don't tell all the girls, but the few of us will go into the city and get lunch my treat. Who does Daniellé want to come with us?" Caleb was great at creating tension in the house by stating and doing outings like this. No one was sure if he did it on purpose or if it was just a natural personality trait.

"Umm…probably me, Amy, Imogen, and Scarlett," Rana whispered while fixing her hair, but Scarlett can't go."

"Very well. Quietly get ready before any of the other girls wake up, and we will leave in twenty minutes," Caleb instructed.

The four of them crammed themselves into the subway car. The great thing about the journey between Brooklyn and Manhattan was that after a few stops, everyone would have a seat. The not so great part was by the time everyone did obtain a seat, it was time to change trains a station later.

The Times Square subway entrance/exit way was always full of hustle and bustle. With buildings reaching up to the clouds, music blaring on every block, and entertainers -even naked ones, dancing across the sidewalks, this part of Manhattan was constantly busy. The girls knew they could not afford to go to any Broadway shows or designer shopping (except for the not present Scarlett) so they were happy just trying on shoes in stores like

Nordstrom, feeling the uplifting atmosphere of Gucci, and doing each other's makeup at the Mac and Clinique counters. For the girls, it was more about the experience than coming home with bags of merchandise. They would have bought all of it if they had the means.

Daniellé smiled widely when she tried on a pair of Louboutin's. She felt like Iggy Azalea, one of her idealized music celebrities, with the techno-colored shoes on her feet. The group cheered her as she did a runway catwalk walk while they sipped complimentary glasses of champagne from the fashion department saleswomen. As a group, they probably looked like the type of women who were married to rich husbands who could afford the merchandise they played dress up and fantasy land. It was by far the happiest moment Daniellé had experienced since the runway show, and she was absorbing all the attention like a sponge. For those moments, she was not thinking about how her aging would affect her modeling career, she was giving herself the opportunity to be truly happy.

A light lunch was exactly that, with the manager watching and covering the tab. Caleb suggested the girls share plates at The Little Apple restaurant to spare the extra calories gained from eating out. Daniellé and Rana split a chicken taco salad dish, while Amy and Imogen split a veggie burger with broccoli. All the models drooled over Caleb's prime cut, eighteen-ounce steak, and cheesy, bacon loaded fries. The four of them could barely remember the last time they had a steak, bacon, cheese, or fries. Imogen was probably the most obvious in her lusting as she leaned in a little too close for comfort to smell Caleb's plate. She received a glare from her manager.

"Weren't those shoes just amazing?" Daniellé commented to the group, still thinking about the colorful masterpieces she wore earlier.

"Definitely! And I adore Kylie's new lipstick line," Amy added, as she looked down at the swatches of color on her wrist glowing from the shiny, brilliant pigments. Rana examined Amy's wrist and nodded in agreement.

"I must be wearing fifteen different scents of perfume from those counter saleswomen. I don't know why they sprayed it in my face. Does my breath smell or something?" Imogen asked.

Giggles spread across the table as the food disappeared quickly.

"We still need to go to a craft store to get your sash and crown for tonight!" Amy reminded the table.

"I think there is a craft store a few stations down from here. They may make them," Rana answered.

"Really? How do you know that?" Amy asked.

None of the girls were that familiar with the city yet, even after a month, and they didn't realize Rana was so familiar with the geography.

"I used my GPS when it was mentioned earlier," Rana lied.

Caleb shot an intrigued look her way, but the other girls quickly accepted the information without further question.

"I'm thinking purple with white letters, like royalty," Amy said. She raised her hands in the air presenting the illusion of her winning pageant days.

"That sounds nice," Caleb agreed. "I will call them now and see if it is an option there. We will get it after lunch. I'm sure it will take them a little time to make it as well."

Caleb stepped away from the table, and the girls felt the tension of judgment leave with him. They ate every bit they could manage before his return. The table was silent, but all faces smiled at each other with full mouths.

When he returned, the remainder of lunch was spent discussing strategy for booking more gigs. Caleb assured the girls that more opportunities would develop after they completed their books, but he failed to mention when that would be or how it would happen when their books were completed. Instead, he steered everyone toward the discussion of how he was in the process of finding alternative means of income possibly starting tonight as a trial run. It was extremely vague at first, but Caleb began providing some more details as he spoke.

"Tonight, is a great opportunity to explore a new possibility for income. If it goes well, we will discuss more in our next team meeting. Vision M.D. is tonight's venue for Daniellé's celebration. Everything should run smoothly," Caleb said.

"I did not realize this was so planned out for my birthday?" Daniellé stated, but it sounded like a question.

"Really?" Imogen commented to Caleb. "Like a club or bar?"

Amy diverted the conversation to a more fun topic, "I have a white sparkle dress you can wear tonight with your birthday things, Daniellé!"

"Really? That sounds amazing! Thank you!" Daniellé replied sincerely.

The table was about to have one of those Brady Bunch moments, but before it could happen, Caleb stood up to declare, "We'd best get to the shop to make sure they have time to make the sash."

As they walked out the door, Imogen told the group that she'd left something at the table. She quickly ran back to the table and stuffed a couple fries into her mouth from Caleb's plate. She smiled at the waitress before meeting the others outside.

Casey's Craft and Designs was written in glittering vinyl letters on the glass doorway of the store. Once inside, Rana and Amy scattered in search of the perfect sash material, while Imogen got distracted by the paint and drawing materials. Caleb motioned to Daniellé urging her toward the jewelry counter near the back of the store.

"So, how does the twenty-one-year-old feel?" Caleb asked, leading the conversation.

Daniellé sighed as her hands grazed over a pair of shiny, costume jewelry diamond earrings. She did not feel the need to continue the stage show for her manager like she did for the other girls. In a way, she felt like she knew where the conversation was about to head.

With more emotion than words she said, "Complicated."

Her eyes flickered to Caleb's face to see his reaction and then back to the earrings.

Caleb gave an understanding smile, but it did not help. "It's not the end yet."

Daniellé did not fully understand what Caleb meant, but she assumed it was an attempt by her manager to encourage her to keep her eye on the prize.

"I want this more than anything. I work hard. I really do. I do not want my age to cause that all to be a waste." Daniellé elaborated as if she was trying to talk her way out of the death plenty.

"It does not go unnoticed. You fight. Most of the girls will not last when things are hard. That type of spirit is difficult to crush." Caleb advised.

Alice and Elise's words of affirmation from their trip to Smoothie King echoed in Daniellé's mind.

Daniellé knew they and Caleb were right, and the others on the management team even said something along those lines when they interviewed her. It still bothered her though.

"What do you think of this one?" Caleb placed a tiara on Daniellé's bright red hair locks.

The only mirror available was a tiny sliver between the sunglasses display stand. Sparkling false diamonds gleamed on Daniellé's crown reflecting various pinks, reds, and oranges from her phoenix-colored hair. Daniellé felt a little bit like a princess. Through the mirror, she saw Amy and Rana walk up behind her.

"Awe!!!" Amy squeaked in delight as she clapped and did a small hop.

Daniellé predicted Amy would grow up to be one of those pageant mom's you see on reality television.

Amy continued in a high-pitched voice, "Here! We think this is the perfect color!"

She gestured at Rana and Imogen to agree again with a nod. Amy draped the unlabeled sash over Daniellé's white hipster overalls and pink sports bra. Everyone approved of Amy's choice of attire.

"Let's get this to the counter to be embroidered." Amy suggested removing it from Daniellé's torso.

Daniellé pulled out her wallet as they walked up to the cashier. "How much is it going to be?" she asked.

"Nothing, of course." Rana said. Rana, Amy, and Imogen began pulling together money from their purses.

"Oh goodness, thank you," Daniellé said flabbergasted by the kindness. "Wow. That is really nice of you all."

They would need to wait twenty minutes for the sash to be ready.

Imogen walked outside to wander around. Amy took a seat next to a bench in the sun, while Rana and Daniellé waited near the counter.

"That girl is a wonder in herself. She is just full of life and does not seem to care what anyone else thinks." Daniellé smiled as she came in closer to see Rana's comment in person.

"Little annoyingly childish, though," Rana added with a critical tone.

"To each their own. She is just a kid after all." Daniellé waved off Rana's comment. "Is something wrong?"

Rana noticed she had been pulling at her white tee shirt. She released it leaving a wrinkled impression.

"I'm fine. Just wanting to get some casting calls and gigs soon. You know?" Rana explained. It was one of the many reasons why she was down.

"Yeah, I get it. I want them too. We all do. At least things are slowly kind of happening. I did not think it was going to be overnight, did you?" Daniellé attempted to reassure her friend and herself.

"Are they happening? Nothing seems wrong to you? Like you think things are still progressing forward?" Rana's voice rose as she spoke.

"What do you mean?" Daniellé asked confused.

"Nothing. Rana realized she was being watched from across the room by Caleb. "Just having some self-doubts, I guess."

The royal purple sash looked elegant with its white letters displaying, "Daniellé's 21st Birthday!"

When paired with the tiara, Daniellé finally understood why women enjoyed the pageant experience so much. She felt like royalty. With the evening quickly approaching, the five of them knew it was time to head back to Brooklyn. The models attempted to catnap hoping to prevent being too tired for the vague but exciting plans of the night. It was also a great time to get online to Model Mayhem and look for modeling submission opportunities. The train ride home was a quiet and quick one. Caleb answered more business phone calls standing apart from the group. Imogen slept, and Amy left her headphones in the whole time.

When they did arrive at the house, no one was there. The remnants of clothing and heels were spread out across the small house.

"Ah. Silence. Beautiful silence." Rana's eyes closed as she embraced the empty house with open arms.

She quickly made her way back to her bunk for her secret snack drawer. Rana was brave breaking the rules. At the bottom of the snack drawer was a photo of her son- a secret she had only shared with Daniellé. Rana kissed it before placing it back under a bag of trail mix and a container of almonds. Following her lead, the other girls went to wash up and rest in the rarity of the quiet place. Caleb walked to the back side of the house to his office and bedroom. There, he made a phone call that could be heard somewhat through the walls.

"Hey. We good?" Caleb spoke quietly into his iPhone.

"Is everything arranged? It must be smooth." Caleb's voice was firm.

"Okay. I will do." Caleb said.

He hung up the phone.

For a moment there was just eerie silence.

"It is a dog eat dog world," Caleb said to himself. "It will be okay, Lucas." It was the first time in months he had used his given name.

The girls were somewhat confused by the conversation, but they shook it off as they drifted off to sleep. In a few hours the serenity of this time would vanish.

Night approached quickly. The house was lively as everyone dressed to impress. The models were instructed to all wear black dresses or jumpers, while Daniellé wore a sequined white, short dress. It was going to be a night to remember as they entered the Uber SUV on their way to the mysterious venue. The building was exactly how people dreamed New York City's best rooftop spots looked. It had tall mirrored walls, gold and silver decor everywhere, and a line out the door. Nine models dressed to the max stepped out of the vehicle to walk straight through the red rope. Two of the management directors, Zane (the newest director responsible for organizing this nightlife event) and Richmond, followed the girls like angry bodyguards.

Envy from men in Calvin Klein suits and women wearing expensive jewels shot through the crowd like a rainbow.

"How much does it normally cost to get into this place?" Amy asked Savannah as she tugged down on her lace black dress.

"$3,000.00 to enter. $10,000.00 to get a table." Savannah winked at the men in line as she replied. Amy gulped as she followed the herd.

"How in the hell-?" Amy asked confused.

"Less questions. More enjoyment!" Savannah hushed Amy in response.

Savannah was not about to let this moment be ruined. This was the type of atmosphere and lifestyle she dreamed about each day.

The elevator went straight to the remarkably beautiful rooftop. A deejay played top-of-the-charts music through a sound system the size of most living rooms. It hung like a canopy over the white booths containing dark marble tables. A long white crystal dance floor divided the rooftop club in half. Its layout was like the model fashion show runways, and men with hand-tailored Givenchy suits danced with supermodels and upcoming celebrities to the beat of the deejay. Silver styled bistro lights draped above while cannon-like fixtures held their position in place from white columns. The floor lit up in neon colors to match the current song's mood. Everything dazzled, amazed, sparkled, and shone.

Scarlett grabbed Daniellé's hand.

"It is absolutely incredible." Scarlett's eyes glistened as she spoke.

Daniellé was at a loss for words. It was unlike anything she had ever seen or imagined. She wondered if New York City was a different planet compared to the rest of the world. It was far better than anywhere else she had seen up to this point in life.

Still everything about it felt like an odd illusion and a little scary, but it was so dazzling.

The models were lead to a long booth beside the V.I.P. section. Their neighbor's section stood a step higher than the others, and their table was not marble, but gold. Bordering the rectangular gold table was the purest white round booth. A venue attendee was lining their area with fresh flower bouquets and restocking the bar above the back of the booth. A centerpiece water fountain began circulating VOSS water.

Rana caught Amy and Imogen staring at the V.I.P. section. "You know that fountain is actually for the creation of mixed drinks. Its water now, but it can be changed to vodka, gin, rum, or whatever on request."

The two models almost believed Rana was lying, but as they continued to stare at their surroundings, they began to believe.

Firecracker champagne glasses were distributed by female servers that wore red dresses and large false diamonds. Each one of them could have easily been a playmate if they tried. The club was surrounded by men in suits with young, beautiful women, while some others in party groups lined the walls chatting.

The whole night went on in amazement and it may have lead into another night of amazement and brilliance.

Amy began hyperventilating and pulled her roommate's arms. Lauren returned the gesture by pulling away with a sour look on her face. Kathleen, more concerned, leaned in closer to see what the matter was.

Breathing heavily Amy almost shrieked while she pointed. "Cody Simpson! I am 99% sure that is Cody Simpson." Rana reached across the girls to push Amy's arm down.

Amy still had the urge to jump up and down. Most of the girls did not know who Cody Simpson was, but for Amy he was a prince.

"You should try to talk to him! Catch his eye or something. " Kathleen eagerly suggested.

Amy in false hope tried to shoot a smile across to the blonde, blue-eyed young actor and music sensation. It was not working though. Instead, she just stared as he laughed with his friends. All the other models except Lauren knew what Amy was trying to accomplish so they too, tried to capture his attention. Nothing. The boy never turned his head in their direction.

"Well, plan B," Savannah suggested with a determined tone. "Come with me, Amy." Savannah smiled.

"I'm coming too." Daniellé added curiously.

Mission 'get Cody Simpson's attention' was in full swing for Amy's sake.

Savannah led the way toward the prince looking boy. Amy stood to her left with sweaty palms and a nervous look on her face. As they approached Cody and his team, Savannah gave him an 'accidental' hip bump as she yelled out, "I love this place!"

While Savannah's arms flew in the air, Amy's thin body tumbled down. Her shoulders and face landed a few inches from Cody's unmentionables. Looking up to see a surprised Cody, she felt mortified. Executives threw out profane language and called for service help. Daniellé had a genuine look of apology and shock on her face, while Savannah gave the crowd her best performance of a look of shame.

Amy pushed herself up from her fall and looked as if she was about to cry. "I am so sorry. I am so, so, so sorry."

She repeated the words five times in a matter of ten seconds. Cody reached down to help the tousled-hair model to her feet. He gracefully pulled a piece of crushed peppermint from her hair with a soft smirk, and Amy almost collapsed right back down to the floor.

"It's okay." The singer flashed his million-dollar smile or did COSMO report it was a two-million-dollar smile?

"I'm Cody. You are?" He asked in a lyrical voice.

"So sorry," Amy said.

Cody laughed. "No, what's your name?"

"Umm…Amy. Please, do not call security on me. I promise I did not mean to do that." She begged with wide innocent, doe-like eyes.

"I would not dare think about it. Hey, everyone. We have company. Meet Amy and her friends?" Cody insisted as he put out his hand for Amy to take. Amy felt a force like the one in Star Wars, telling her to take his hand, so she did.

She turned to see Savannah smiling at her. Daniellé looked extremely worried.

"Savannah! And this is Daniellé. Let's party!" Savannah smiled.

Amy's eyes begged Daniellé to stay with her too, and Daniellé caved once again to Amy's innocent begging look.

"Wow. We are going to be in so, so much trouble. This just happened," Daniellé said under her breath.

Two executive-types slid apart to make room and then instantly placed their arms behind her and other girls at the top of the booth. Daniellé attempted small talk with a very nervous and eager businessman.

"Mission accomplished," Amy whispered to Daniellé.

The drinking that night led to an intermingling of events so that sequence times and occurrences couldn't be understood fully. The time spent with Cody Simpson could have been spread out over the course of the night, but it's best described as all one event. In that haze, perhaps the events surrounding Scarlett happened the night before, the night of, or even after their actual meeting of Cody Simpson. It is all just blurred, and Daniellé's recollection was pieced together from a mixture of sources. In the venue, Scarlett and another model approached the bar and asked for a couple of drinks from the stash the server was prepping. They were handed amber fluids.

"YOLO!" Scarlett yelled the clearly outdated term as she chugged the drink down like a shot. "Now, I really will need to pee!"

The two of them waited in line for what seemed like twenty minutes. When they finally could see the restroom keeper in sight, Scarlett was swaying in her heels.

"You do not drink alcohol much do you?" The other model asked.

"I do. I mean I don't. I…do not like this type." Scarlett said slurring her words.

"Next!" The restroom attendant shouted. Scarlett lunged forward to meet her new best friend the restroom stall. After five minutes, the other model asked Scarlett if she needed any help.

A begging Scarlett replied, "Yes, please." The other model entered the stall to take the short model's hand. Leading her to the mirror. Scarlett was repulsed by her image.

"Let's get you out of here. I will text Caleb and say you are not feeling well." The other model suggested.

Scarlett leaned heavy on her friend's shoulders as they led her out of the building. Bystanders saw them and assumed she was the classic party girl who went too far. Even the men who would typically break their necks to be near the two angel-faced women, turned in disgust. The two of them might as well had been invisible in the crowd. No one noticed. No one cared.

Even the elevator attendant stuck his nose up at the girls.

Across the room, a sparkling firework birthday cake for Daniellé appeared with six server girls standing around the table dancing and cheering. Cody suggested they take a drive down to the Empire State building where Drake would be meeting up with them. Daniellé had no clue who Drake, Rocky something, or Cody were until that night, but Amy begged for her to go along. They had both received a text saying that if they stayed together and told the agency where they were going, they were free to stay out until 4:00 a.m. So, they did just that.

At the top of the Empire State building in her pageant attire, Daniellé felt more alive than ever. She stood almost Titanic-style on a raised area away from the smaller more intimate party crowd. She just smiled as she captured the city wind and gazed upon all the lights of the city. It felt magical and surreal. A man approached her from behind with a sweet smile and Canadian accent. He wore a C.E.O type suit. But Daniellé just kept gazing upon the city in wonder.

"It is so incredible. So, beautiful. It makes you forget everything, everyone. The past. The future." She described to the stranger who was barely taller than her.

"I think it is the past like yours and the past like mine, that makes two people understand one another." The stranger said in a lyrical tone. Daniellé turned to face the man. He had milky dark skin with a brightly lit smile like Charles Michael Davis from that vampire show. In all reality, the alcohol could very well be making a man who was a six look like a nine, but she was okay with the illusion.

"So, what is a woman like you doing up here alone?" The beautiful man said in a deep voice.

"That was cheesy. I am trying to remember a perfect moment to the beginning of my dreams. Cheesy answer for a cheesy question." Daniellé chuckled as she replied. She felt weightless and at peace in the madness of her life. She was at her birthday's peak.

"May I try to add to such a moment?" The stranger took a step closer to the phoenix-haired princess as the wind tousled her hair.

Her green eyes were intensified by the background of city lights, and her dress glittered brightly. She appeared as a bright angel standing next to a dark, mysterious beautiful man.

Her heart raced as his soft hand slide up her cheek to push back her hair, and his arm kept her from losing her balance. His embrace was firm enough to keep her from fainting, but gentle enough for her to want to press against it. She knew it was insane and crazy, and against her better judgment. She knew she should say, "No." She knew all the horror stories of kissing a stranger, but she nodded yes.

She whispered, "So, cheesy. Go ahead."

On the night of Daniellé's twenty-first birthday, Daniellé's dreams of adventure and beauty were heightened by the unknown kiss of the one and only Drake.

Section Two: Go-See

The ancient Greeks believed diamonds were the tears of the Gods. When everything shines, dazzles, and sparkles in the world of New York City's fashion industry, the eyes may seem to be filled with a thousand bright, blinding diamonds. The only thing strong enough to scratch a diamond is another diamond.

Perhaps, if the signs had been known or clearer. If educational tools could have provided some highlight to the subtle red flags of a well-organized stream of events. If someone would have wrote this story before it had a chance to occur. Then perhaps Daniellé too, could have been strong like a diamond.

Lighted, Magnifying Mirror

To understand a story such as the models of a Brooklyn house, it is worth revisiting the beginning. Taking it from the top, gives one opportunity to fill in the missing puzzle pieces and spot the red flags. Imagine the difference between putting on makeup using a lighted LED vanity magnifying mirror verses doing the same thing in a dark room. The application is completely different, and the results of the dark room effort can be very scary.

In pure and blessed fiction, all the answers to the difficult questions can be provided. Characters can be all-knowing, and most of the time the good guys are destined to win the battle. In this story, the best version of the truth develops from multiple sources with the best information collected from mixed ears and voice. In this story, the answers are not always understandable and a bit discombobulating. Therefore, here in the story of these beautiful Brooklyn models, the goal is to present the best possible recollection of causation, correlation, and the consequence of events starting with the GAL Agency hiring interview with Elise's documentary.

Elise had left in high spirits ten or so minutes ago after accepting her new position at GAL agency. The directors, Caleb, Richmond, and Zane had been discussing the interview amongst themselves since Elise's departure. Zane was the type to stay out of heated topics, but Caleb and Richmond were in a full-on debate. These people had one thing in common, they liked to make money — lots and lots of money. Caleb and Richmond were not seeing eye-to-eye on the best inventory and methods to make the lots and lots of money.

Richmond was clearly unimpressed as he thought Elise was as an amateur. He did not bother hiding it as he announced it during Elise's panel interview.

"I am not comfortable with her. Why hire so quickly?" Richmond asked.

Things began heating up as Leviathan Redwood, a tall slender copper blonde, walked into the room holding a few glasses of water.

"You know I can hear you two from the elevators, right?" Leviathan stated in annoyed frustration.

Turning to Zane, "What is their problem today?"

Zane was one of those chill dark, club-atmosphere types and the most charming of the group with his blue eyes and blonde hair. If hip-hop was playing and a drink was in his hand, he was happy. Twiddling with his phone he acknowledged Leviathan with a shake of his head.

"Look, they just hired this new film intern. Caleb likes her. Richmond doesn't. Not my territory." Zane informed him with a careless, shrug.

He was right though. New hires were not under his umbrella of responsibility. The job responsibilities had to be clear for everything to go according to plan. Leviathan handled finances, Caleb covered talent coordination, Zane ran anything nightclub-related, and Richmond handled anything else that needed to be done. Between the four of them, GAL agency was the newest well-oiled modeling agency in New York City.

At least, that was the story they pitched.

"Well, she is hired. Besides, we may have options," Caleb explained to the group.

Richmond scoffed at the statement. "Fine. She's your responsibility."

The four of them ran down their checklist of hired models and their dates of arrival. Each had comments about their favorites and even more comments on the ones which they disagreed on. The list consisted of women between the ages of seventeen and twenty-three, at least 5' 9" tall, and skinny as rails. The perfect group of *modelesque* statues for high fashion. That was the idea they sold to each one of them, no matter where they were traveling from in the world. GAL agency was going to provide them housing and, and perhaps, the pathway to their dreams. After all, if someone can make it in the Big Apple, one can make it anywhere, right?

"Leviathan, do you mind reading out the list for us as of yesterday's updates? I have completed so many interviews. I am losing track of which girls we actually selected," Caleb requested.

Between the four of them, they had sorted several applications of aspiring models. Leviathan pulled out some manila folders of the approved candidates. There were going to be about twenty to twenty-two models living in the house at any given time. A bountiful of talent potential, but the story could be spent focusing on just ten models and maintain this story's purpose. These models would be traveling from all over to live in the model house under GAL's jurisdiction.

Even if they happened to be from the same regions by chance, none of the girls knew one another. They had more in common though than just aspiring dreams in the fashion industry, pretty faces, and small tiny framed bodies. They all had mainly soft personalities. Like most young woman, they had their fair share of insecurities. None of them were rich on their own, but one or two were dating *well*. Each of them had some type of tragedy in their past, (death of a loved ones, divorced parents, orphan, various versions of abuse etc.) that they wanted to keep secret, but all ten of these women still had hopes of a bright future. They were willing to take a leap of faith on a tall tale.

"Let's only go through the first set for now. Savannah Giles. She is from Los Angeles and part Norwegian too. Height 5'11", hair, short and blonde.

She describes herself as a peaceful individual who enjoys surfing at the beach and yoga. Great." Leviathan explained.

Caleb chimed in, "I immediately thought 'commercials' for her."

"Okay, good. Who is next?" Richmond asked.

"Rana Vera. She's from Argentina. She has lived in New York City for the past ten years. Height 5'11", hair, curly and black, eyes, brown." Richmond and Zane shared an impish glance.

 "Next is Calista Ahmann. Standing at 6'0", she lives in Los Angeles, right now. She has olive-toned skin and describes herself as a lobbyist. Wow." Leviathan turned the photo to show Calista. "She looks like Vogue material, for sure."

I told you, I only choose the best," Caleb stated confidently. "After all, I only do prime meat."

"How about you take a swing at naming off some of these girls Richmond?" Leviathan insisted as he handed the folders to Richmond. "It will help you become more familiar."

Richmond stood. Clearing his throat, he looked at the next headshot. It was Lauren McCleanan. Taking a step back, he said "Are we sure about this one?"

"Her bone structure is strong. She's unique. She's got strong features," said Caleb rolling his eyes at Richmond.

"I am not sure unique and tough looking fits with our overall goal. We want bombshells, not- bombs," Zane voiced an opinion in a jokingly manner.

"Hush, Zane. Geez." Caleb protested.

Caleb grabbed the next folder. With a mocking pageant voice, he introduced the next girls rather quickly to move the meeting forward. "Imogen Crockett is from the Keys. Both her hair and skin are pure white as snow."

Everyone nodded in approval as Caleb continued, "Amy Willington is our fitness model. She is 5'9" with blue eyes. Next is a real-life Barbie named Kathleen Stone. She has platinum hair down to her hips and blue eyes. I remember she had a very soft voice on the phone." Caleb stopped and sipped his coffee.

Zane picked up the three remaining folders. "Okay. So, Scarlett Lumbers looks a lot like Adriana Lima. She is a lot shorter than the other girls though. I thought the cut-off was 5'9"? It says she is 5'6"."

"Honestly, does it matter?" Caleb questioned. "She is going to be the first to be outsourced. Think promotional."

Zane clearly understood what she meant and continued to the next folder, "Bebe Standifer looks like another beach chick. Blonde, pixie cut hair, with blue eyes and a tan. Lastly is Daniellé Winters. She has hair as red as a phoenix and green eyes."

All four members of the team looked satisfied, absorbing all the knowledge of these wishful models currently traveling to New York by car, train, or plane. Each one of them eager and nervous to start their lives in the Big Apple: Savannah Giles, Rana Vera, Calista Ahmann. Lauren McCleanan, Imogen Crockett, Kathleen Stone, Amy Willington, Scarlett Lumbers, Bebe Standifer, and Daniellé Winters. Each one ready to become the next modeling sensation, but not a one of them prepared for what GAL agency had in store.

Long Island. Quick Changes.

Daniellé reflected on the early morning conversation that occurred a couple weeks after the Couture Fashion show, with her roommates circled standing around the kitchen. The topic was food, of course, and they were on the hunt in these scarce quarters. Funds were tight around here, and GAL agency thought the first thing to cut was the food. In last night's house meeting, they mentioned cutting food costs would help both the numbers on the scale and the numbers in the budget. It was a jab that resulted in a collective glare of anger from a house of rail thin models. It was like management couldn't realize the reality -the largest model in the room was all of 125 pounds.

Bebe found half a box of wheat thins. Calista and Scarlett had a leftover Subway club sandwich to share, and Amy and Kathleen had bananas and oatmeal. Hopeful, everyone looked at Imogen for what she'd brought to the table. She added a half empty jar of peanut butter and licorice whips to the collection.

"This is just sad," Danielle said.

"We need real food. I'm calling that pizza joint down the street." Savannah commented. She left the kitchen to find her cell phone.

"What about food stamps?" Bebe mentioned.

The room turned around looking at her like she had lost her mind. Most of the girls here had pride engraved in their souls along with Prada, Gucci, and Galliano. So much so that it might as well be engraved in the soles of their shoes as well.

"What?" We need food." Bebe said defensively. "Surely, one or two of us qualify. It is the United States after all."

Most of the girls landed small gigs like a photoshoot for a local designers or businesses. Even Daniellé had trouble finding work since the fashion show. It did not help that Daniellé was using most of her money to pay off her student loan. She had thought putting money toward her debt was good advice from Dave Ramsey, but now as her stomach rumbled, she felt differently. The others were not talking about their latest paychecks, perhaps because they were becoming rarer.

Daniellé had resorted to hair shows in Long Island for extra cash despite the warning from GAL agency about changing her hair. They did not bother to ask what the changes involved. Sometimes, Daniellé would just come home from a fishtail braid tutorial or hair conditioning treatment.

At the very least the jobs got her out of a house full of hungry, frustrated estrogen. Not much starts a fight quicker than hungry people struggling to earn a buck. Some of them even asked about getting part time jobs at nearby restaurants or coffee shops, but it was frowned upon from the managers. They were told to stay focused on modeling gigs only, but it was hard to stay focused when bank accounts dwindled.

"You are right," Calista admitted. "Let's consider it."

Bebe and Calista pulled out their phones to search the web.

"No one here has any dependents, do they?" Bebe laughed as she asked presenting it as a joke.

Everyone looked down at their phones waiting, but one of the girls had a worried, troubled look in her eye. Truth was, no one really knew much about their roommates. The modeling contracts told them to keep their personal lives on the down low and additional conversations stressed keeping their personal lives confidential. Management was all about non-disclosure.

Each of the models wanted to share more about their worlds, hometowns, and previous booking experiences, but it was not worth the stigma of GAL's disapproval. Of course, gossip and other things flourished in the limited topics available. Even Daniellé wanted to tell someone about her confusing possible new crush, or perhaps the fact that Daryl had not returned any of her phone calls in weeks. No fights had occurred, but he seemed to reply to her messages less and less frequently. Daniellé did not understand why he was distancing himself from her, and it was just so lonely not being able to speak to anyone. For the redhead, it was like she was more isolated from the world as the days continued.

Topics like food stamps and the struggle of the last couple weeks had to be done in hushed voices. Caleb was constantly pulling aside individual girls to warn them not to trust the others when it came to their careers or divulging personal information. Most of them found it odd to be in a house of selected talent in which management did not even trust.

Daniellé constantly felt hurt by the information shared by Caleb. She considered some of her roommates as friends, and it felt like those were always the ones Caleb said spread the worst of lies and rumors. She, along with the others, had begun to question if it was the roommates or management they should be wary of trusting.

Daniellé had left for Long Island shortly after the kitchen conversation. It was a temporary escape from diet restrictions, workout slots, chores, behavior restrictions, and curfews. Lately, Daniellé had noticed she got a lot of freedom when the management team did not benefit from her hair shows. They had told her to be thankful they did not require a percentage from these assignments. Perturbed, Daniellé knew they did not book her, escort her, process payment, or do anything in relation to the gig. In fact, they did very little lately toward bookings.

How is it any type of favor? I do all the work, and they reap the benefits. She thought.

GAL agency was doing zilch, zero, nothing lately to help her book gigs or obtain casting opportunities or go-sees. They seemed more interested in her and the others playing the waiting game, but she applied to every booking she could find online or through networking. If the agency's main goal was to establish working models, one would think they would be pushing harder toward auditions. How else could they get paid or expect the models to be able to afford living in this expensive city?

The Long Island train reminded Daniellé of that books where the boy wizard headed to that magical school. She had never actually read the Harry Potter books in their entirety, but she remembered her younger brother discussing the details of the Hogwarts train back home. Daniellé was not good at keeping up with mainstream media, especially lately given her other needs. She was educating herself on the self-promotion and service business practices of the fashion and entertainment industry, but the internet was her main teacher.

In front of a wooden bench in the boarding station, she stood with a boarding pass ticket in her hand along with the other passengers. When the train arrived, in some subconscious directed synchronization people stood up with their suitcases and newspapers. One might have believed it was the early 1930s with the formality and promptness of the communication between the ticket master and passengers as he punched a star into Daniellé's ticket stub. To her, it was like the beginning of one of those romance adventure novels.

The only downside was the hour and a half commute because there was no direct transportation path. She had to travel to Penn Station in Manhattan by subway before she could make her way up to Long Island by train. The New York City subway system was very discombobulating for someone non-local. She did not mind Penn Station though. It was lively and occasionally celebrities, like Miley Cyrus, would roam the underground singing in disguise.

Traveling to hair shows felt like small vacations when everything else was a muddle in her life. She knew she would need better solutions pronto.

Daniellé worked for two days that week as the talented hair artist's, Stephanie Eds, muse. Stephanie was a graduate of the Paul Mitchell Hair Institution of Staten Island, but they had been covering the state and country with private hair shows for select salons for a variety of different brands. Daniellé thought it was a neat concept, and along with payment she always got hair supplies like shampoo and conditioner in between the sessions.

"Maintenance is everything with flaming hair like yours, girlie." Stephanie would advise each time before Daniellé would leave.

Stephanie was a down-to-earth good ole Cajun. It was clear to see how observant Stephanie was both inside and outside of her work. The hair artist explained every minute detail to Daniellé and the audience. The audience had a wide range of experience levels from investors, to beauty students, to experienced salon owners like Stephanie. Great with words, Stephanie had the ability to talk like a pro and yet make everything easy enough for hair beginners to understand. She knew her business inside and out. Each show delivered a great lesson for the viewers, and Daniellé, like a knowledge sponge, was saddened when the session was over.

Daniellé dreaded leaving this session as she seated herself for the ride back to Brooklyn. The train whistled to signal its departure back to Manhattan, Daniellé reviewed her day at the hair show while looking at her new shinier hair.

Stephanie explained in detail the hair transformation process as she pulled up a cafe lounge chair for Daniellé. They had been working together for a few weeks, therefore Daniellé knew Stephanie liked to review what would happen before the doors opened. She did this just in case anything in Stephanie's session might make Daniellé uncomfortable. Stephanie elegantly tousled Daniellé's hair from above her chair, she moved it around to create different parts in her hair and styles.

"I'm thinking brighter tones and then we finish with a lesson on waterfall braiding for the audience," Stephanie commented to herself.

Daniellé remembered how the first time she participated in a hair show Stephanie would ask her opinion about the lowlights, but now she knew better. That was a mistake that left them both in awkward silence for ten minutes or so. Danelle's model release covered minor changes and cuts to the hair, and Stephanie was mostly asking Daniellé out of courtesy. At this point if Stephanie did not cut it all off or make it purple, Daniellé went along with it.

Stephanie's hair was virgin-type, meaning that no previous coloring had ever been applied. Daniellé was very surprised by the jargon at first. Stephanie Ed's mane was a curly, natural red reaching all the way down to her hips. In the first hair show, Stephanie had every strand of it straight-ironed. The model was amazed at how healthy the hair was and how long it was, reaching beyond the hair artist's buttocks. She also imagined it would be difficult to sit or manage hair so long. Nonetheless, as a result, she felt comfortable in the Cajun's chair. After all, if anyone knew about hair care it was the real-life version of *The Little Mermaid.*

"How are you liking the hair show seminars?" Stephanie's voice sounded deep southern.

"It is very informative and fun," Daniellé replied with a smile.

As a professional talent, any deeper conversation beyond small talk with the client is not encouraged. Daniellé had read the advice in a modeling book when she first started. Daniellé typically talked too much, so she kept this at the forefront of her thoughts when she was with clients or other talent. In fact, the horror stories the agency told her about the interactions between clients and talent made her extremely nervous to talk at all.

Daniellé, at this point, trained herself to be polite and keep the conversation light, and if possible to be as innocuous as she could. She remembered one of her model friends from the house joking, "Models are meant to be seen, not heard." She laughed as she recited the motto.

Stephanie smiled at her talent widely with approval. "Daniellé, you know you are welcome to any of the food in the cafe by our vendor. I want my model well-fed, even though it does not look like you eat much. There is plenty."

Inside, Daniellé's heart was jumping for joy despite the slight offense to the "not eating" comment. Did she really say Daniellé could eat and that there was plenty? She did not even know what stood behind the doors of the cafe, but it must have been God-sent.

"Of course, we will have to make this R.E.D 10, first!" Stephanie instructed.

Daniellé tried to keep her eyes from lighting up like a Christmas tree when she sheepishly asked, "Thank you very much, but are you sure there is enough for the crew and me?"

Stephanie's laughing reply was thick with deep southern accent, "Of course dear. Besides, I saw how you ate that breakfast lemon square when you arrived...If I had to guess you most likely have not eaten in days. Kidding, of course." Step laughed as she spoke.

Was she? Daniellé thought.

It was a bold deduction by Stephanie, but a true one. Daniellé's jaw dropped with the daring statement.

Daniellé wondered. *Is it a Cajun thing to say exactly what came to mind or was she just being overly sensitive?*

There was no way Stephanie could know times were tough for Daniellé financially. They barely spoke about anything beyond hair products and Biotin supplements. This was one of those moments Daniellé's sensitivity needed to be silenced. After all, models were meant to be seen, not heard, right?

A sense of shame washed over the red-headed girl, and Stephanie's demeanor changed as she realized she might have offended her talent. Daniellé remained quiet as she looked at the reflection of her frail physique in the mirror. It was apparent that she was not eating according to a dietitian's recommendations. Despite the malnutrition, the scale was not budging as much as Daniellé wish it would, but starvation works a little differently than healthy dieting.

Stephanie, attuned to the new surrounding aura, changed the mood with a hearty laugh. "Eat as much as you wish, and I will have the black coloring cape over you for the remainder of the day" she said.

With two collected smiles, Stephanie began her work.

When the hair show was finished, the model walked into the cafe. Many faces turned to evaluate her fresh new brighter tones, but all the model saw was the bountiful amounts of catering sandwiches, pasta, and desserts on the long table.

Long table. Ha. Long Island. Daniellé cracked herself up.

It could have been Thanksgiving with all the food that was laid out before her. Bashfully she looked around the room for a place to sit holding the largest plate of food she had seen in weeks. Every bite was delicious, and she had not been this excited for a ham sandwich in her entire life.

Daniellé stashed some oatmeal cookies away to eat later. The meal, fresh look, and last week's paycheck left her smiling all the way home. When she finally arrived, she met Scarlett and Savannah on the roof to soak up some rays.

"When are you going to talk about it?" Scarlett asked Daniellé.

Scarlett, Savannah, and Daniellé laid out on the rooftop with towels separating their bodies from the asphalt surface. The rooftop gave them a little more privacy and space but even more importantly – a tanning opportunity. Most of the girls were frightened by the height of the ladder reaching from the third story, but these three found their dislike for heights to be of their advantage.

Models Stop Traffic • 100

Daniellé flipped over onto her stomach as she unraveled the top of her swimsuit. It was her way of avoiding tan lines, but Daniellé's skin was not the type to really tan in the first place. She used what seemed like a pint of sunblock a day, but she was mainly up here to feel the sun's heat on her skin. Her oversized hat and sunglasses looked out of proportion to the rest of her body. In opposite side of the spectrum, Savannah loved soaking up the heat of the sun on her oiled skin. It was not the beach, but it was an okay second best. As far as Scarlett's intentions, no one ever really had a clue – perhaps she just liked the social aspect of it all.

"Never," Daniellé said.

Scarlett and Daniellé seemed to be having a secret conversation that made no sense to Savannah.

In close quarters like these, it felt like telepathy became a real thing. Daniellé knew exactly what Scarlett was trying to discuss, and it was not going to happen. First, because she did not know why Scarlett really wanted to know, and second because it was just complex chaos. Daryl had continued to dodge most of Daniellé's phone calls, and his texts only revealed signs of his busy work and friend schedule. Daniellé did not realize that her moving to New York City meant Daryl was going to be a missing in action jerk. Usually, she would not stress about her love life- even one as complex as theirs. Typically, she would be contently sleeping at night, but this situation with Daryl, had her head spinning trying to figure out the problem. It was one thing if she had done something wrong.

It was another thing altogether if he was ghosting her for no reason. Besides, aren't ghosts supposed to haunt you, not disappear?

She understood that she was the one who left him physically, and that decision was for her career, passion, and life goals. She was foolish to believe he understood and supported her. Perhaps, he did not think she would like New York City and run home? Perhaps, he thought she would be unsuccessful and give up right away? She had a million possible situations running through her head, but only one reality. Daryl was distancing himself from her, and she was not doing as well as she hoped. She craved the emotional support he provided back home. She, in a way, needed him – if nothing more than she just needed a friend.

"Suit yourself," Scarlett said as she carelessly pretended not to care. "So, anyone know the important topic they want to discuss at the house meeting tonight? What is it about?" Scarlett lifted herself to her side facing Savannah and Daniellé.

Savannah's headphones had her occupied with Bob Marley, so Daniellé gave her a slight nudge to get her attention.

"Yeah?" Savannah shouted above her music.

The girls laughed in amusement of Savannah's lack of awareness about the world around her.

"Yeah, you know or yeah as in yeah?" Scarlett asked just to add to the confusion.

"What?" Savannah replied.

"Do you know what the house meeting is about tonight?" Daniellé asked again.

"Oh yeah, something about promotional work for money between gigs." Savannah's comment only provided more questions than answers.

"Like handing out flyers and samples? I used to do that at malls for perfumes." Scarlett added.

"No, like nightclubs and hot spots in town. Money-follows-beautiful-people type of thing." Savannah corrected.

Scarlett and Daniellé both pondered. Daniellé had never been one for the club or bar atmospheres. In her first three years of her college she had only experienced two clubs (which she regretted), a few frat or house parties (which she regretted), and bars in which primarily served food (which she did not regret so much). Scarlett on the other hand, was used to the Stereo Nightclub and The Drop Lounge in Chicago or even the clubs of Malibu or the Hamptons. All three girls held completely different ideas of what it would be like to work in the promotional atmosphere of a nightclub, but none of them had it right. That became very clear at that night's meeting.

Brave

It stormed furiously outside as the directors and models gathered into the common area for that night's household meeting. Calista was running late. Everyone was gossiping about her repeated lateness after the first few meetings. The managers were clearly unimpressed with any of her excuses. Once, Calista, said she was late from a working out at gym and lost track of time, once from a subway breakdown, and another time from a Manhattan casting call. The last excuse was understandable to most of the other girls, but the prior two excuses left a bad taste in the management team's mouth. No one knew yet why she was running late this time, but the management team told her that her late arrival would have severe consequences.

Lately, the models remaining had all seen models fired from the agency for the smallest of reasons. It made them afraid that they could be next. Not to mention, that there was a certain stigma that once gone, they should not affiliate with the fired models anymore.

The team meetings primarily focused on the opportunity of upcoming group calls, if any, or the portfolio shoots, if any. Most meetings also discussed living arrangements and chore lists. However, this meeting was rumored to be about a new stream of revenue.

"Okay, everyone," Caleb announced calling the meeting to order. "As you all know, a lot of changes are happening. Of course, auditions for New York Fashion Week are right around the corner, so hit the gym extra hard in the next few weeks. This is a great chance to be noticed and signed by a good agency. Not everyone will get signed with Elite, Ford, or Wilhelmina, but there are still other lesser known agencies that provide good work for models. So, keep working hard."

Caleb nodded in his own affirmation as Richmond stood to address the group. His demeanor was less jolly.

"As you all know funds are important to maintain the prestige look as a model and part of GAL agency's roster. As stated in your contracts, we are not responsible for income, but Zane has decided to help with work at some popular nightclubs in Manhattan. We know that many of you have not done any promotional nightlife work before, and none of you have worked as promotional models in the nightlife atmosphere. Therefore, it is vital that you pay attention to everything we say and tell you to do. You won't be paid for this directly, but other compensation will be provided like your rent and some food."

Zane handed Amy some printed instruction handouts to pass out to the other models. Around the room was a sea of inquisitive, worried, and excited facial expressions.

Daniellé looked down at the paper handed to her by Rana. Her face was a blend of the inquisitive and worried. She noticed that Rana's face looked like she had been crying, but Daniellé thought it might be her allergies acting up again. After all, allergies were big in New York with all the industrial pollution. Daniellé was lucky in this regard as part of her childhood was spent living in the Great Smoky Mountains, and her father pretty much bled orange in support of the University of Tennessee Vols. The handout itself was more like the Ten Commandments than an informational pamphlet. Daniellé skipped over the introductory formalities, and read the rules about accepting the promotional modeling job:

1. Models will abide by a strict schedule each completing 2-3 nights, *at least*, of promotional nightlife work in the employers chosen or alternating venues (including the possibility of multiple venues in one shift) from a flexible time between 10:00 p.m. to 2:30 a.m. unless otherwise discussed, models cannot change in shifts with other models. Note this does not include travel time.

2. Each model will be required to meet a certain level of "look and appropriate appearance" while attending the venues. (i.e. Full glam style makeup, Fixed hair, Jewelry, Nightlife Dress Attire, No Flats, No Jeans, No Ponytails, No Chipped Nail Polish. Etc.)

3. A driver or member of management will escort you to and from the venue. No exceptions.

4. You are not to talk to anyone at the venue unless instructed by management.

5. No Eating. No Drinking, unless provided by management. Some alcoholic beverage choices will be provided at the venues by management. Use at your discretion.

6. Do not leave the venue's table without a provided escort unless otherwise instructed.

7. Limit your time talking to other models during the shift. You will be joined by other models in GAL agency's care not residing in the home. Dancing is allowed and encouraged.

8. Arrive with a good attitude and maintain a happy and smiling demeanor throughout the shift.

9. Do not leave the venue. If an emergency occurs, alert management.

10. Upon completing all the designated promotional shifts for the month, your portion of rent and household food will be paid for you as payment. Please note, you may be asked to cover for other models if needed, and this will be part of your quota. This does not increase your stipend but is a general courtesy to your housemates.

The list gave Daniellé a queasy feeling. In a way, she knew she needed the income and resources if she was to stay in New York City to pursue modeling, but she was not the party nightlife type. She much rather preferred reading a good book on finance or attending a local play with friends. The idea of famous rappers and girls gone wild dancing on tables played in her mind from music videos. For the first time she analyzed the actions of the women in the videos more than the singers. They were like arm candy, but she did not morally agree with all the sexual actions affiliated with the lyrics in the video. Were those girls too just trying to earn money in a tough world, or was their actions truly just because they had very different personalities than Daniellé? After this thinking, Daniellé only had one question she needed answered. Could she act the part long enough to be financially stable and not affect her moral standards?

"So, just three nights a week for a few hours?" Lauren asked hesitantly.

"It depends on the number of models that agree and the needs of the household," Leviathan replied. "If everyone agrees then it should only be three nights a week with the help of our out-of-home models."

Rana had already agreed and handed the paper back to Richmond. With a slight smile, he lifted the paper.

"When you're ready, turn them into me unless you just choose to keep it for review." Caleb announced.

Kathleen's face looked like she felt the peer pressure. Daniellé felt herself tense up, and the Barbie's breathing changed pace beside her. The redhead looked up trying not to be noticed. Looking to see if her eyes expressed the same concern in Kathleen. The two of them read the paper over a couple times more as Calista walked into the room. The management team collectively shot her with a disappointed and frustrated scowl, as the tardy model she sat next to Kathleen and Daniellé.

Daniellé's heart raced a little faster, but she was unsure if it came from the situation's intensity or Calista's presence. Savannah eagerly handed Calista a paper to inform her of the topic of discussion. The beach babe's face was full of excitement at the new opportunity.

Calista, the late raven beauty, leaned over to whisper to Kathleen and Daniellé, "Is this for real? I thought we were models, not club bunnies?"

Neither Daniellé nor Kathleen had heard of the term "club bunnies". They gave Calista a puzzled look.

"Club bunnies. It is like the 'Entourage' for rappers and executive businessmen. That way they can feel important and desired. It is like glorified escorting." Calista explained in a condescending tone.

It was clear Calista did not approve.

"They said we would not have to talk to anyone while we're there, and it would possibly pay for some household food and rent," Kathleen added.

"Yes, but are we required to do anything *beyond* stand there-maybe dance a little? I do not like the idea of being an escort or something like that." Daniellé asked.

"We have these types of venues in Los Angeles. Back home it is more like an escort service. They tend to want a little more than dancing, babe," Calista looked at Daniellé.

The color Daniellé's face started to match her hair.

Calista continued as she switched back to Kathleen, "I came here to be a model. Yes, I want to have fun, but be a model not anything else."

Their conversation gathered many intrigued looks from the room, including management.

"Is there something wrong? We are just trying to find a way to help bring money into this house. None of this is free after all. It is a business. You all are being very disrespectful to the rest of the group." Caleb butted into their conversation making it more public.

"No, just reviewing the paper as a group," Daniellé replied holding it up.

All the other girls in the room except these three had given their consent. Perhaps they were desperate for income, or maybe these three girls were overreacting. It just felt so odd. Over the past few weeks, it felt like the agency *wanted* them to be distressed and worried. They had told them not to take part-time jobs. What made this so different?

The other models waited for them impatiently so that the meeting could either continue or conclude.

"I will give this to you after the meeting, so that I can ask questions without taking up anyone else's time." Calista smiled politely, but it was not reciprocated.

It sounded like a reasonable and professional approach. Perhaps management was still too perturbed by her late attendance to reciprocate a kind gesture.

"Very well. We can collect them afterward and answer any questions. That is all we really had to discuss. You missed most of it by not being on time." Richmond stated harshly.

It was an odd sentence to say when the topic of nightlife venue work was only the second topic of discussion in the meeting. They had only spent a few minutes discussing the day to day mundane issues. Richmond's eyes did not go to the side of the room where Kathleen, Daniellé, or Calista sat again.

When the house meeting was called to an end, everyone but the three models, Caleb, and Richmond scattered to their corners of the house. Zane and Leviathan said their goodbyes as they left, and Zane started dialing a number on his phone to make a business call. They asked Kathleen and Daniellé to stay nearby to answer any of their questions about the income opportunity. Caleb paused and turned his face toward Calista. After a locked stare, Caleb asked for her to leave the house.

"What do you mean?" Calista replied dumbfounded.

"I want you to leave. You're fired." Caleb elaborated. "You have been very unprofessional tonight and in the past weeks, and we do not want your influence in this household anymore.

Not again. How many models does that make it this week? She was late again, but is this necessary? Daniellé worried. *How many had been fired now?*

Calista stood up, and furiously said, "I am the best model here! I have done nothing but work my ass off since the moment I landed in New Work. You all have not done anything for me or the other girls' careers. This place is a joke!"

Daniellé's heart hurt from the first comment, and Kathleen's face looked insulted and appalled. Daniellé felt stupid for thinking so highly of Calista, and believing she thought highly of her or the others.

Daniellé's thoughts continued in a rush around in her head. *Did she really think she was so much better than everyone else? Sure, she was the woman you would imagine posted on Times Square billboards, but all the other girls were beautiful. Surely, she is just hurt or angry, right?*

Kathleen and Daniellé shared a look of disgust about Calista's words. Hearing that distasteful note, the others opened their doors and peeked out to listen to the rest of the conversation and its next direction.

"It is that attitude exactly why you will no longer be working with us." Richmond commanded.

He seemed assured that the other models were officially on his side.

Calista fell silent as she noticed the faces of her peers.

The models of the house were all jaw-dropped. The termination meant she had to pack her bags now and leave. There would be no downtime or time to arrange next steps. When a model was fired it meant immediate removal. Quietly but quickly, Calista grabbed her clothing and suitcases from her room. The thing with having such little living space meant your bags were always half-packed. Calista did not speak or look at anyone as she gathered her belongings, nor did any of the household roommates attempt to talk with her as it happened. Caleb and Richmond went into Caleb's room for a discussion.

Ten minutes of complete silence passed in the household. Daniellé leaned against the wall near the front door debating whether to talk to Calista before she left. Daniellé was conflicted with concern, pain, and anger.

Two blue suitcases rolled up with Calista.

"Where are you going to go?" Daniellé asked quietly.

"A hotel, I guess. Then I will do what I came here to do-model." Calista's voice was agitated.

"Do you want to talk tomorrow? Maybe I can try to talk to Caleb." Daniellé regretted the offer immediately, but her hand still reached for Calista's hand.

"No. I do not want your help." Calista's voice sounded cruel as she pulled away.

"I just thought…" Daniellé replied.

"It does not matter what you thought. It means nothing now." The gap-toothed model said sharply.

Daniellé pulled her hand away and drew her long cardigan tightly around her waist. She straightened her back and fought back tears. Calista saw the hurt on her face, but it appeared she was trying to maintain her own composure.

"Look, I will call you in a couple days. Promise." Calista assured her with an apologetic look.

She opened the door, and Daniellé closed it slowly. Relocking it, Daniellé leaned back against it. Her conflicted state was even more heightened.

Calista completed two trips down the flight of stairs, one for each suitcase. Finally, she reached the iron gate outside. Sunset had passed an hour ago, and the moon had taken its shift in the sky. Most likely, tears started rolling down her olive-toned face and were caught in her raven hair as she reviewed the current events in her head. Could she accomplish her dream all alone?

Ten minutes later Daniellé walked outside to talk to Calista, but she was nowhere to be found.

Lights. Camera. Action.

Another emergency group meeting was scheduled for ten minutes later. Gossip ran across the walls of the house, but the subjects changed like a shuffling card deck. Elise and Alice talked in the kitchen with Bebe and Lauren listened. Each of them twiddled about trying to look oblivious to the conversation at hand.

"Her name is Flora. Like a flower. Or is that her stage name?" Elise said as she rushed to setup her cameras.

"Stage name. She does not know any English. We might need to get Daniellé to help us interview her." Alice suggested.

"Great idea if she is willing to help. I have been pushing off her part of the documentary for weeks. I am not sure she will help with someone else's interview. People tend to be bitter toward that type of thing."

"Why have you not completed it?" Alice asked amazed. "Don't we need that for our footage, like yesterday?"

"Yeah." Elise stared at the equipment.

Everyone flooded into the common room. Caleb and Richmond closed the office door behind them as they approached the common area. Caleb wore a Chanel pant suit, and Richmond dressed in a purple suit with a white tie to complete his ensemble. Their clothing was the only colorful clothing to be seen the room as it was becoming standard practice to be in model attire at all time. It was like a psychosocial uniform had influenced the models. It was the model's way of being the same height, weight, shape, and dress. It was a drastic change from the rainbow of color, patterns, and textures worn when they first arrived. Now, it was simple. All the girls wore a plain black tank top and black leggings to match. The most variety was if they wanted to wear nude 5-inch heels or black 5-inch heels.

"First off, we have a busy day today, so I hope you all have prepared yourselves. Second, we are very disappointed in you all as group, and third, we'll get into it." Caleb called the meeting to order with a snarl on his face.

Most of the time meetings were held late at night after a hard day of work, but it was barely 6:00 a.m.

The yawning heard across the room only made Caleb more temperamental. "First, as you know one of your teammates has decided to break several rules you agreed to in the contract each of you all signed when we became your managers. While we have still yet to hear from Scarlett, if you want to call her a lady, when she is reached she will be immediately terminated from GAL agency and this household. This is in addition to Calista and others. They are not permitted back in this house." Caleb said in an assertive, almost threatening tone.

Everyone shuffled uncomfortably.

Richmond decided to announce the next big news: "A new model will be joining us from Paris today. As she only knows French, we thought it would be best to have her in Daniellé's room. You know French, right? Please welcome her on our behalf, and help the others communicate as much as possible. More importantly, for you all is your runway training today with Rihanna's backup dancer Coco. She is an amazing artist that will be able to teach you all the essentials of body awareness. After that, I believe several of you have castings or bookings today. For the three of you that do not, you all have been alerted to work on something."

The meeting continued for twenty more minutes with repeating scolding about the behavior of the models. From an outsider considering the situation, nothing they did overall as a group was that horrific. Sure, some of the girls left shoes in the living room daily, but nothing too crazy. Compared to most model houses this was the ideal scenario, but GAL had other idea about it.

All eight of the models felt like scolded puppies when the meeting was adjourned. They cowered back to their rooms with their tails between their legs, metaphorically of course. It was not until the door closed that the girls voiced their opinions to their roommates.

Savannah started, "Damn it. Why did Scarlett have to go mess everything up for the rest of us?"

Kathleen sheepishly added, "Perhaps, she just drank too much?"

Lauren said in her normal tone, "In the two minutes that we were there? Really? She can't just be a typical slut?"

Savannah laughed at Lauren's comment, "She cost us."

"I think-. Scarlett was just the excuse they used." Amy said as a rebuttal.

Lauren agreed with a nod.

A group sigh traveled around the room. Silence covered the room except for the outside traffic as they packed their purses with their practice runway heels. Savannah broke the silence.

"Do you think she is legit? This Rihanna woman?" Savannah asked.

"Ha! Did you really just ask if Rihanna is legit?" Amy winked.

"You know what I mean!" Savannah protested.

"I looked her up. She is the real deal. Pretty exciting. How did we manage to get it?" Kathleen chimed in. The mood lightened with the knowledge of being officially trained by one of Rihanna's top choreographers. Once everyone was ready the group headed out.

Traveling as a group of ten was no easy feat, and when the models saw Alice and Elise at the front gate, they knew it was going to be even more difficult. One of the rules was to stay together. It was on the long list along with "do not talk to anyone besides each other". The micromanaging was starting to cause a little insanity. After a long subway trip to upper Manhattan, the group walked five blocks to a skyscraper that looked like every other skyscraper in New York. Tall. Silver. Reflective. The only real difference was this one had the number 0602 in calligraphy on the glass window.

"This is it," Amy announced to the group.

"Is it just me or does our group shrink in number by the day?" Alice asked as she held the door open for the others.

"It makes filming easier, but it really is a story killer. How will there be any footage left at this rate?" Elise whispered to Alice.

Alice agreed with a silent nod. The models were not unaware of what the film crew was thinking. That was one reason why the interviews became shorter and shorter, and Elise relied more on the behind-the-scenes footage.

Three elevator trips later, the models walked into a studio with chairs lined horizontally across the ballet studio-like floors. There were eight chairs to be exact, but no choreographer. Each of the girls took a seat, and somewhat awkwardly gazed into the mirror at one another. They were used to studying their own angles in mirrors at home, but this was a genuine side by side comparison of each other. Each of them found themselves coveting another's features.

Rana wanted the manageability of Kathleen's long locks. Amy wanted Rana's long eyelashes. Daniellé wanted Amy's extremely toned arms, but Amy wanted Daniellé's extra-long legs. It was a brutal cycle of insecurity. Models are like that though. They seem like the most gorgeous, confident women to the outside world, but inside they are the most insecure of us all. Think about it. They must be perfect every single day. They must be the ideal, and they never get a day off from the judgment that encircles them. They attend casting calls on Monday telling them they are too fat, round faced, big footed, and that they hate their hair color. Then on Wednesday they are told by different judges they are too skinny, square faced, but their hair color is good. If that kind of confusing feedback didn't cause some emotional whiplash, what would?

The staring contest was brought to an abrupt halt when a loud 5'1" bodacious dancer strutted into the room. She wore heels almost as tall as the beach bag she walked with, but she walked gracefully.

"Hey, my play dolls! You ready to work it today?" She announced to the row of chairs that held her audience.

She continued. "Because I am KQ, and we are going to work you! Up on your feet. You can't do runway sitting down!"

The models sprang up as they moved the chairs out away from the middle of the floor. Perhaps, it would have been more practical to have not had those in the middle of the floor.

"So, we are going to work it to my girl Rihanna. I want you all to line up and show me what you are working with." KQ instructed.

Bebe and Kathleen looked stunned, Savannah jumped with excitement, and the camera crew could barely keep their composure as they tried not to laugh. The only one that felt even halfway confident to walk first was Daniellé, and the other ladies pushed her to the front. KQ started the training with a click of her IPOD and Rihanna's "S.O.S" played. Most of the room felt the comic relief and irony of the scenario.

Daniellé tied up her hair in a messy bun, and shoulders pushed back as she walked down the imaginary runway. KQ stood at the end. Her face was filled with half judgment and half satisfaction as Daniellé cat walked. Daniellé's natural look was fierce. That was almost a given with the phoenix red hair and intense facial features. Her confidence only rattled the other models that had to follow her. She even gave the Candice Swanepoel's signature wink at the end.

Model after model walked to Rihanna's beat. KQ shut off the music and stood to address the eight of them. Her air of dissatisfaction filled the entire room as she scanned the frail looking bodies of the group.

"So, how many of you all have walked in a runway show before?" She asked in a sassy tone.

A few lifted their hands nervously. Models are used to being judged at every corner they pass, but something about KQ's judgment made them uncomfortable.

"I see. You bitches walkin' like a crocodile is going to come up and bite you!" KQ shared in a loud voice. "Take control of your territory. You walk it. It doesn't walk you. Now, try again with some confidence."

None of the models understood where their source of confidence was supposed to spring from after that insult. They lined up again.

And again. And again. And again.

They lined up for five hours straight watching their bodies move down the ballet studio through the reflections of the mirrors. They analyzed hip placement, posture, facial expressions, and even the count of their steps to the end. By the end of the five hours, KQ's voice was shot, Bebe and Rana's feet bleed, and shin splints developed in most of the trainees. After what seemed like the 4th time through of Rihanna's album, they all could match their stride to the beat. Most importantly, they felt S.O.S.

"That's a wrap! You girls looked hot that last time through. Nice class. Keep up the work." KQ's speech was not all that encouraging to the group.

Even Elise and Alice had snuck out quietly two hours into the repeating cycle. The extra time was going to allow her to review this week's footage sooner, and interview Flora before the French girl met the other models. Elise was thankful for Google Translate.

Of the group only Daniellé, Imogen, Lauren, Amy, and Kathleen were invited to the casting for J.Q. Collections. J.Q. Collections was an incredible bridal designer known far beyond the streets of Manhattan. Right up there with Vera Wang and David's Bridal as the most coveted gowns for new brides. The girls were told to wait in the lounging area for the executive administrator to meet them.

"Oh! What pretty, pretty models we have here!" Said a 5'6" man in a J.Q. suit with a high-pitched voice as he approached the group. "I'm Chandler Singer! And yes, I love to sing! Line up! Let's look!"

It was becoming second nature for the girls to line up. They had developed an innate order and everything. In this case, it went Lauren, Imogen, Daniellé, Kathleen, and Amy. Chandler with his pointer finger on his lip envisioned the girls in the available gowns. Everyone stood silently for two minutes. The models were stone still, but it felt more like waiting for a preschool girl to choose which Barbie's to play with.

"FABULOUS! 2,4, and 5 go to the secretary out front! Ask to be directed to fitting!" He directed. "The rest of you can go home. Thank you for your time." The casting was quick. Chandler did not even ask for them to walk.

Lauren scoffed. "Can you tell us why?"

Daniellé answered her, "It is because we just do not fit what he needs. I have flaming red hair and you are too edgy."

Chandler smiled at Daniellé. "Yes. It is nothing personal."

Lauren gave them both sour looks as she walked out alone. Daniellé shook Chandler's hand, gave him her comp card, and escorted herself out. She knew better than to burn bridges. This was a lesson that Lauren was still learning.

Lauren decided to take a stroll across central park. It was very rare she had the freedom of a few hours to herself. She was seriously considering quitting this whole modeling thing. She had only traveled to New York for the free summer vacation, and her boyfriend back home was threatening to break up with her if she did not return soon. She decided it was a great time to call him and talk it all out.

Daniellé hopped right back on the subway station to head home. It was not that she was upset about the casting call, in fact, she was used to people either loving or hating her appearance. She took out her copy of RUSSH and began studying the poses.

Before Daniellé could open the door, she heard shuffling. She placed her ear to the door. She recognized the sounds, but her mind did not understand who or they could be? She opened the door as quietly as she could. She was in top spy mode as she peaked around the corner. There she saw a sight she immediately wished she had not. Two people engaging in one of life's most primal practices. Thrust after thrust, the woman did not appear to make much noise.

Daniellé covered her mouth trying not to vomit.

This was so wrong! The rules?! Sex? Is it sex? She leaned around the corner of the hallway to look again.

The woman appeared to be silently crying.

Do other women cry during sex? I do not think this is sex. Is it? Damn it! Daniellé thought. *She left noiseless and escaped to the rooftop.*

Daniellé clutched at her throat gasping for air as she begged and pleaded with her thoughts. She had recently discovered she was more religious now than she ever was in North Carolina. As her knees pressed down into the still lukewarm roofing of the Brooklyn apartment, tears contributed to the swelling of her eyes.

"God." It was the only word that seemed to escape Daniellé's small lips.

Models Stop Traffic • 126

Daniellé was typically a strong individual. She was tough like her mother in bad situations, and she had the intellectual gift of problem-solving like her father. Ever since she was a little girl Daniellé dreamed of being in front of the camera and walking down that runway.

The words, "Lights! Camera! Action!" Were inscribed in her DNA.

For a girl who came from small town USA, most people did not understand her love for the big city. They would write it off as a 'phase I was going through' or 'Daniellé's new fad'. Even years later they thought it was just a 'young' thing that she would grow out of eventually. Here at twenty-one years old, it was the longest phase she had ever experienced. While her family did not understand it back home, Brooklyn natives shared the passion and the competition.

So, why was all this happening?

Why were all her dreams turning into nightmares?

How could she even begin to react to witnessing what she had?

Did she witness what she thought she truly had?

A few hours ago, the biggest competitors she knew where the ones living with her or the models outside these walls. Now, could they be the one's managing her? She had moved to New York to chase dreams, but somehow this was her modeling world now.

Sex? Rape? These lines are so blurred. Daniellé thought.

The life of "you are never going to be tiny enough" and "let us dissect you in a line as you walk" was hard enough but now?

It is her life.

Ask her?

Would that be wrong?

Embarrassing? Could it have been a sick foreplay game?

Maybe this has been going on the whole time?

No. It could not be.

It just can't.

It just looked so off. Daniellé's mind raced with thoughts.

Being alone in the concrete jungle could be the best aspect and worst aspect of these last few months. Daniellé's personality was extremely independent, and the fact that she was brave enough to chase her dreams gave her a sense of pride. But now, she would give anything to feel her mother's arms wrapped around her.

As Daniellé's head tilted toward the sky, the clouds fogged up her view as dusk began to approach. After about fifteen minutes of choked sobbing, she was ready to finally talk to God about what she had witnessed. Sadly, like most of Daniellé's prayers, she began with an apology for all the wrong she committed lately. She wondered if what she had just done or did not do, counted.

Certain aspects of modeling and acting introduced a multitude of sins, for instance, your body is not always treated like a temple. After apologizing for all the nightlife and such, she began to talk to God about how Daniellé felt lost. She did not trust anyone the way she once did, and her heart was losing compassion for others. The Daniellé who once would give her last dime to someone was now becoming the cutthroat hustle of New York City. Loving thy neighbor seemed impossible lately when everyone around Daniellé was architecting her downfall.

Was that girl just trying to rise to the top as well? She thought.

That type of pressure can really mess who someone's psychological makeup. Some of the statements from Caleb's voice haunted Daniellé's dreams. She knew not to listen, but his leadership position made it hard for her not to obey Caleb. Daniellé wanted to stay in the house, after all, so she tried to filter out all the cruel comments, lies, and manipulative statements Caleb told her and the other models. With all the shady and unprofessional events happening, it was no wonder Daniellé felt like she was losing focus on the reason she left home for New York City. All

Daniellé could hope for was that the pros always out-weighed the cons. If the cons ever became too heavy, Lord knows what she would be left to do.

Wait. Now, the cons *did* outweigh the pros. Now, she needed the Lord to tell her what to do.

As Daniellé kneeled on the asphalt roof, she looked off into the cityscape view. If she squinted hard enough she could see the city buildings in the far distance. This was absolutely mesmerizing to her, especially the way they had lit it up in red, white, and blue on Independence Day a few weeks ago.

Daniellé thought. *How can you have all your dreams laid before you, and not feel tricked or used, or scared?*

Daniellé was finding out so many lies and hidden facts about GAL agency that she was not sure if any of the great things happening lately were a reality. Caleb's strong voice kept ringing in her head, "It is a surprise!" That was the answer to everything the models asked. Daniellé was never one for surprises.

Perhaps, there was a deeper reason behind the surprises.

Daniellé should have known from the beginning that following a passion blindly was a bad idea. When is it ever intelligent to do anything unknowingly? Consequences are very real, and as time went on she realized how naive being blind can make you.

Her first surprise was the idea of promotional modeling. When GAL agency said the models would be required to do 9 to 12 hours of promotional modeling, Daniellé believed it was a legit way to earn some extra cash. Instead, it was the opposite. It felt deeply wrong. She could not explain it, but there was something about it. She could not even share it with her parents or friends. Something about it felt dirty.

GAL's definition of promotional modeling was standing in nightclubs from 11:30 p.m. until around 4:30 a.m. Each of the models was obligated to work three to four times a week. The contract only said nine to twelve hours, but if a model complained about the process she would either be targeted for more hours or fired on the spot. Daniellé's mind returned to the thought of Calista. She pulled out her phone to message her but put it away quickly.

Daniellé's mind still raced with thoughts. *Cold shoulder? Wait, is it really the cold shoulder? Was it really sex? Did Scarlett really take off for no reason? Where are all the other girls that keeping taking off?*

Thus far, the nightlife promotional modeling had not bothered her. It seemed very sketchy, but it was overall bearable. Now, Daniellé began to really think about it all clearly.

My friend Ginger used to be a model, and she told me that legit models have curfews of 8:00 p.m. for model houses. She remembered.

Had times changed, or should the models of the house be concerned that shifts began at 8:00 p.m.?

Then there was the drinking and whole atmosphere of the nightlife. Daniellé was not a clubber back home. In fact, there was not a bar within forty miles of her house. So, going from nothing to the top clubs like Tang and ROCC was giving her whiplash. The excitement had dazzled her eyes with stardust.

Could businessmen really spend $10,000 on a table for just one night? Just to be surrounded by liquor, loud music, and a skyline. Her brain analyzed deeper and deeper. I will admit that the ROCC skyline was breathtaking, but I did not really think it was worth $10,000 for a cheap overcrowded table? Why do we go there, exactly?

Daniellé was not feeling much like a model anymore. She didn't even remember much of who she was or what she stood for in the past. The model version of herself had no identity. Something in her heart told Daniellé that this is was not the industry she dreamed of when she was growing up. It seemed tainted and diseased. Was this real what the fashion industry included, or was Daniellé just in a situation where she had not really been modeling, to begin with?

Her soul felt a presence of evil intentions surrounding her. She could not label the feeling quite yet, but it reminded her of a child scared of the dark. The part of Daniellé that was in love with fashion wanted to tell herself to relax, that this must be some sort of paranoia.

Daniellé held her head between her knees. She rocked back and forth. The air never reached quite down to her lungs.

Daniellé's mind just repeated. *What to do? What to do?*

"Tu n's rein?" a voice behind her said.

Daniellé turned, scared to see who was speaking to her. At the rooftop door stood an angelic woman half way up the entry. Her skin was milky tan, and her voice was soft. The question was coming from a French girl of trocadéro style.

"Tu n's rcin?" she repeated. "Ça va?" She looked frustrated that she did not know the words in English. She did the thumbs up, thumbs down gesture toward Daniellé.

"Je parles français et je vais bien," Daniellé replied that she knew French and that she was fine. The eyes of the French girl lit up.

"Je suis Flora." Flora introduced herself. She took a seat next to Daniellé. Daniellé did not immediately reply. She continued to just look forward searching for the cityscape beyond the clouds.

"Enchanté, Flora. Enchanté." Daniellé's voice was barren.

Backfire

The lights remained off as Rana, Imogen, and Daniellé stood in their bedroom at the model house. Light seeped through the hallway as Rana was in a frenzied panic. Imogen and Daniellé stared at Rana as she frantically packed her suitcase. A few moments before, Imogen had shared the recent group conversation from the subway. A group of the models in the house had attended a sketchy casting call arranged by GAL agency all the way out in Harlem, and because of a tragically unofficial casting call, they had questioned the legitimacy of the agency itself. There seemed to be more fogginess and questions concerning the professionalism and connections GAL had to the fashion community, if any. Secondly, the girls had begun questioning the legitimacy of the individual manager's credentials as well.

Daniellé recalled some of the questions from the group in her mind. She cycled through them attempting to find answers, but she fell short.

Daniellé thought. *Why haven't we heard from the girls who were fired? Didn't Caleb mention something about Calista prostituting herself out in the night clubs now? Not even a text or a call. Aren't we down like five models this week? Does this mean we have to go out to those nightlife events every night to compensate since our numbers are down?*

There was no apparent or reasonably proper explanation. When they arrived back at the model house, Imogen and Daniellé met up with Rana to see if she could help. She seemed closer with some of the managers than most of the others, but it seemed to backfire quickly. She wanted to be logical, but her dreams of being a top model were getting in the way. Without GAL and this house, her time in New York City would end abruptly.

"I am not staying another minute in this place. You see what is happening?" Rana continued packed her bag furiously fast. Clothes and shoes flew across their tiny room, and Rana was not even entirely sure whose.

"I am leaving. You need to as well. This is exactly what Calista talked about, perhaps worse! By the way, anyone else notice half the house is empty? Did we all really hate each other that much? Social media? No. And not all of us were even friends on social media. This is insane." Rana's words were confusing in her hurried speech.

"Things are fucked up, yes. But let's at least try to think logically through it." Daniellé said pointlessly. "I have a private investigator friend I can call. He can do some background checks on these people and company."

Imogen nodded in approval at Daniellé's idea, but Rana paused for half a moment to stare at them before continuing her packing.

"Look, you all do not know this, but I talked to Caleb. Did you know that he is related to another team member? Cousins. We do not even know their real names. How are you going to research them without that?" Rana's words continued to race out of her.

"What are you talking about? Real names?" Imogen's innocent face looked puzzled.

"Why are you just now sharing this? How close are you all?" Daniellé asked surprised and unfulfilled.

"Because I also *smoked* with them, thus breaking the house rules. Quite frankly, do not act like they have not shared things with you secretly. Both of you!" Rana defended herself.

"Yeah. Like Caleb has a thing for the show Mad Men. Not that his name is not really Caleb! What are their names then? And who is related to who?" Daniellé demanded to know.

"That is not the point. The point is I need to get out of here now." Rana insisted as she pushed off the inquisition.

"Not without answers!" Imogen insisted with the imaginary strength of the Bubble's Powderpuff Girl.

Daniellé's mind was still reeling from the last comment. This was all happening too tremendously fast for her mind to process.

Rana was not waiting around to explain any further. She began zipping up the bag, and she placed one hand each on Daniellé and Imogen's shoulders.

"Please, come with me. This place is dangerous. They are involuntarily or maybe even voluntarily using the others as escorts or something else wrong. They are selling us out in one way or another. And honestly, I would not be surprised if we never hear from those other girls again. Maybe it is about trying to make a quick buck before they sell off those girls to the highest bid at those nightlife events. Maybe that is the bid? Who knows? But I am not staying here one more second to find out." Rana's voice now cracked as she began to fight a crying fit.

Daniellé stared into Rana's terror- eyes. She could see that Rana knew more about the situation and their managers than either she or Imogen did, but Rana was not sharing.

"Why not just tell us?" Daniellé asked.

Silence.

What the hell happened? Is she scared to talk to us or something? Daniellé thought.

At least, she was sharing *something* here and now. Daniellé glanced over at Imogen to see the same fear in her eyes and shaking body. She wanted to just pull the both into a tight hug and say, "It is fine. There is a solution here. We just need to put our minds together to find it." She could not though. Like them, she had no clue.

"Let me give this all to the private investigator. I do not want to throw this all away if we are misunderstanding." Daniellé whispered to the two girls. "I can call him right now. He is really good."

"You aren't coming with me, are you?" Rana asked coldly.

Silence.

Daniellé looked down at the floor.

"I need to talk to my mom." Imogen answered weakly.

Rana stepped away from the redhead and blonde and out of the room. It seemed like only half a second had passed when they heard the front door slam shut.

Fight or Flight

The day after Rana ran away.

Lipstick painted models walked in and out of rooms of the house. With Rana now gone, all the models of the house were expected to attend the nightlife club tonight. For some of the girls this was the third night in a row working the nightclub shift.

Does rent really cost this much? Daniellé thought as she slid on the six-inch black heels.

It was becoming more and more difficult to cover up her sleep deprived eyes. Working at night gave them the opportunity to attend castings and gigs in the daytime, but since they were exhausted it was quite impossible to look fresh. By morning, all she and others wanted to do was sleep. It was terrifying to talk with the management about Rana's sudden departure. They began asking what had happened and where Rana had gone as if Daniellé held the answers.

"Are they concerned for her safety or some other reason?" Daniellé thought during what felt like an interrogation each time Rana's name came up in conversation — which was every conversation with management.

Models Stop Traffic

Despite the high traffic in the small area of the house, no one chatted. Perhaps, all Daniellé's thoughts were the same as the other models? It would explain the piercing silence.

The car ride to the venue was just as silent as the house. The managers had given Daniellé permission to start driving the models to and back from their nightlife events. It was something Rana previously held as a chore. They made it seem like a privilege, but driving was Daniellé's least favorite activity. GAL had recently decided, it was cheaper having the car handy for a shift instead of constantly supplying a taxi.

No one cared for rap or any music tonight, but a couple models whispered in the back seat. It was just meaningless gossip about the previous models of the house: Scarlett, Calista, Rana, etc. Daniellé really wished for a mute button right about them.

Since Daniellé's birthday(s) celebrations, the models were joined by more promotional girls to maintain their numbers. They tended to be of Ukraine, Asian, or Russian decent, and no one in the house knew the connection GAL agency had with the other models. There possibly could have been additional model houses. It made the nights even more awkward. Little was said over the course of four hours when there were language, rule, and culture barriers.

Typically, the night scene of Manhattan is one of brightly colored, loud music fun. Tonight, it was a customized prison for Daniellé. She observed the patrons closely. For the first time she noticed other groups of promotional teams joining their group. The other models looked rougher and older than the girls standing next to her. Some were snorting different drugs and others were drunkenly dancing with men in suits. Each time before it happened, a club member would walk up to a group's leader.

It was odd, and it was calculated.

It was wrong.

When vodka and other drinks arrived at their table, the girls of the other half of the promotional team picked up their drinks first and consumed fast. Zane handed one to Daniellé, she smiled sweetly, but as soon as he turned away, she placed the drink on the floor next to her feet. She wanted to be clear of mind. Perhaps a drink was the reason she was had not detected so much information before this night.

She watched the repeated actions of the other groups around her. A man or woman would walk up, suddenly the model would be dancing away or leaving the club. When these men approached Zane, the conversation was much longer than the ones across the room. Perhaps, there were more details or other conditions involved. The men still pointed at the models as if selecting at a butcher's shop.

This night was full of surprises as Caleb had decided to attend. Occasionally, he would be lost in business conversation with Zane. The club music was always too loud to hear anyone's speech without a direct connection to the listener's ear. Caleb looked stern tonight and it concerned in the models' attitudes. Fake smiles and mouthing of the lyrics continued each time Caleb told them to look more lively and happy.

An hour into the night, Caleb approached Daniellé. His mouth moved closer to her ear as he asked to have a word with her. Daniellé's eyes widened at the thought, but Caleb was too close to tell. All Daniellé could do was nod yes. It was almost like a spell had been cast on her. Some psychological conditioning prevented her from saying anything in refusal.

She followed Caleb outside of the club. Daniellé saw the lines of red roped patrons begging to be let in to have some fun. Daniellé was always shocked at how so many people could not only afford dropping a couple grand on a table, but also willing to wait outside for hours. There was no guarantee of getting inside -unless of course, you were a celebrity or knew someone important.

Daniellé began to shiver in her short dress and black designer heels. Scarlett had left them behind, and Daniellé felt a little closer to her when she wore them. The managers never approved of any of Daniellé's personal wardrobe. They even went as far to buy some cheap club like dresses for a community closest.

"So, Rana's gone." Caleb started the conversation.

"Yeah." Daniellé replied. She was not looking forward to another interrogation.

"Let's go sit in the car. You look like you could catch your death." Caleb insisted.

Daniellé did not really think he was asking by his choice of words. She led the way with the keys between her knuckles. It was something she learned from a stranger on the subway. Even though Daniellé walked toward the driver's side, Caleb insisted that he sit in the driver's seat. So, she took the passenger's seat. She left the door slightly open hoping that was not where this was heading.

Caleb began talking again.

"She was my favorite, you know?" Caleb asserted.

"It does not matter now." Daniellé tried to act indifferent to Caleb's comment.

What does he mean by favorite? Favorite what? She thought.

"We connected. I really had high hopes for her." Caleb continued.

"Then should we be looking for more casting calls instead of nightlife events?" Daniellé questioned.

She immediately wanted to retract the statement. Caleb held her left wrist firmly now.

"You are all just spoiled brats from privileged homes." Caleb announced.

Tugging for release, Daniellé said. "Did you even read my papers?"

Each of their eyes were locked hard onto one another's. They were like two spiders with raised legs trying to measure up their opponent's threatening stance. Daniellé could not break free of his grip though.

Kick open the door and scream. Kick off the shoes and run. She thought.

Caleb released her wrist and returned to his hand to his side of the car.

"Sorry. I am just upset." Caleb apologized and released.

"Aren't we all…" Daniellé responded. "How about the six or so others? Have you heard from them?"

Daniellé decided to tread carefully, she was in red flagged water. She was either being incredible brave, incredibly dumb, or both.

"I think Calista has gotten herself caught up in some trouble with some of the others. I do not know about Rana." Caleb answered.

"What type of trouble?" Daniellé pressed the topic.

"Not sure. Have not heard much of it." Caleb answered.

The two of them sat in dark silence for a while. This was not a conversation of concern, but they were analyzing each other. They were trying to find out more about what the other person knew. Daniellé held her gripped arm close to her to display weakness. It was a tactful thought, which may or may not have been working. Sitting here with Caleb was like sitting with Adam in the airport. She was scared, but that darkness she had in her, it was real. She knew it. She knew she was willing to fight if it came to it. At the same time though, she knew how scared she was. She always had to push herself to be brave. Back home, her friends described her as fearless, but she was fearful. Something inside of her let her still push through in the face of the horror. She wished it was the battle against stage fright or calling a crush instead. This fear had the potential to cause much more than a bruised ego.

"Well, I should probably get back inside. Numbers, right?" Daniellé said with a fake laugh as she spoke.

She pushed up the car door to get out, but Caleb's arm pulled her back inside the car. Their eyes locked again, now, was the possible moment of her reckoning.

Run. Run. Damn it. Move. Daniellé begged herself.

Her eyes stayed locked onto Caleb's returned gripping hand. She looked up to see what seemed like a cross between s look of worry, agony, and panic on Caleb's face.

Why does he look like he is the one about to be beaten? Daniellé thought. *What trouble is he in with Rana's leaving?*

"Let go of me." Daniellé hissed.

Her phoenix hair reflected in the dim lightly. She felt powerful in that statement. Perhaps, she would take the "fight" in the fight or flight response. Caleb recoiled again.

"I will find her you know. I have to find her." Caleb said.

Daniellé wanted to know why, but she wanted to be away from her manager more.

"I want to go back in. I do not know anything." Daniellé asserted.

"That is a lie. You know where she went. You all talked non-stop." Caleb demanded.

Daniellé had finally made her way out of the car. She could hear people not too far off from them. In New York City, it was a hit or miss on if pedestrians helped one another. It was like the bystander effect nine out of ten times.

"If I am a liar, then it doesn't matter anyways. I am going back." Daniellé announced.

Caleb exited the car and locked it with a click from his key set. He handed Daniellé back the keys, but his hand just lingered in midair.

"I am sorry. Perhaps, I had one too many. I know none of this is your fault." Caleb apologized again.

Daniellé took back the keys. If for no other reason than to have a weapon if he laid another hand on her. She knew Caleb was lying though. He had not taken a single drink from the table when the server made rounds. Perhaps, he was hoping she would have been the intoxicated one.

"We can work on this more tomorrow. Figure it out together." Caleb suggested.

Daniellé looked at him with a flat look on her face as she began walking toward the club again. It was a quick, silent walk and an immediate re-entry.

Daniellé approached the group with a flat look and frantic mind. They had been drinking, but that was not what shocked Daniellé. She looked at the other promotional groups. The contrast was not as apparent as she had originally thought. Some of the girls she did not know were taking *hits* of whatever they could get their hands on. They all had been drinking- some even danced.

She didn't.

She felt nauseated.

She felt anxious.

She wanted to cry.

But she could not. She turned off all the emotions she could. Tonight, her eyes were open.

Her phone buzzed from the private investigator's text.

"We need to talk. This does not look good." Gabriel wrote.

Danielle fought back tears as she tucked her phone back into her bag:

Her mind cried. *I want to leave.*

If You Can Make It in New York

The day after Daniellé's car conversation with Caleb.

Daniellé's friend, Gabriel Thomas, had found very little in the legitimacy of GAL Agency. It was not because he was not good at researching these type of situations, but there was just not much *to* find. Gabriel, a man in his early thirties, had seen his fair share of odd and sketchy circumstances, but this one was perplexing. Being a well-known politician and public figure, he used the available resources and tactics he knew to help Daniellé. Their connection over the years had grown from a mentor/mentee to a big brother/little sister. So, when his research felt like falling down a rabbit's hole, Gabriel quickly became concerned for Daniellé's safety. He was not in New York City to analyze the situation, but Daniellé would have not called him if she was not truly worried.

Daniellé liked to create the illusion that her life was like a fairytale, so revealing something as dark and frightening as this situation was happening, was a huge leap outside of her comfort zone. She could not avoid it anymore though, not after last night's tense conversation. So, she told Gabriel all she knew about this place, these people, and what had happened lately, and when she did that, she felt like she knew barely anything.

She provided the website link first. Gabriel explained websites reveal additional information beyond their first general appearances. The information here revealed the website was created just a few weeks before her arrival, and the site was connected to another company. Not just any type of company though, it had to be one that made Daniellé's skin crawl. The connected affiliate company specialized in escorts and promotional modeling services. Daniellé gulped hard at learning this truth.

They acted like they had been working in the fashion industry so much longer, and promotional modeling at night venues was new to them. Daniellé thought as Gabriel shared his discoveries.

The private investigator also explained there was no physical address associated with the website. This was a confusing topic as he tried to explain how things needed to be rooted somewhere. Even the address labeled on the website was not a real address. Daniellé thought back to a time she had seen what was supposed to be the GAL headquarters. All she could remember was being in a conference room somewhere in Manhattan for less than thirty minutes.

I am so naive. She thought. *Surely, they should have shown us something beyond a long conference room table.*

Daniellé felt like an idiot, but Gabriel continued to share. She always assumed that the address at the Manhattan office was the same as the website. Then again, she had only been their once, and it could have easily been a situation where they rented the room out just for the occasion. The office could belong to a friend of a friend or perhaps it was the office of a different company entirely. Daniellé found herself trying to come up with better explanations. Gabriel said he understood why she felt like she had to come up with excuses, but the facts were being laid out in front of her. She just needed to accept them.

GAL agency said they were running a different type of process for this set of models. Daniellé thought they meant an approach on how to reach higher end modeling agencies or the type of models they selected for their process. Now, she felt like it was a different approach to a different type of business. Perhaps the one Gabriel had connected with one of the managers.

It got worse though. He searched and searched for the names of the management crew. He avoided social media platforms at first to find a professional manner or setting. He quickly discovered that the owner of the website was someone Indian, but Daniellé did not recognize the name.

"Anyone can create a Facebook, Instagram, or Twitter page, after all. I am looking for public records connected with the government or such." Gabriel explained.

Daniellé provided every piece of information she knew about where any of the three of them called their hometown or they had previously worked.

No hits.

Now, she was as terrified as Rana had been.

Could Rana have known this? Surely not. She would have never stayed if she had. Ha. She did not stay. Daniellé questioned herself.

The closest connection was a shared name connected to a different man in the state of Delaware. The man was dead though as of the last few years.

Daniellé's mind went to an eerie place as her heart began racing.

This was all being revealed quickly, and she was angry none of this was shared previously. She had been sent up here, but what had she been sent up here to do, exactly? Prior to the call, Daniellé climbed the ladder to the rooftop for the privacy of the phone call, but now, she just wanted to fall off it. She felt like she already had.

How could I be so stupid? Seriously, this can't be happening. She thought desperately. *Is nothing real? Why can't I explain any of this?*

"It feels like someone just walked up to my head and shook it like a Magic Eight-Ball." Daniellé said. "But there is no answer coming out. It is just all so conflicting and all the answers...they just cause more questions."

"I'm sorry, Daniellé. But we should really take some more steps here. You don't know anything else?" Gabriel asked.

Daniellé told him about a couple of events and photoshoots arranged by management. Gabriel searched as she patiently waited. It was easy to tell that he did not like causing Daniellé enormous anxiety, but she needed to hear every detail.

"Perhaps, they paid for a couple things like that to keep you all distracted? I mean do they seem more focused on evolving your career or something else?" Gabriel asked.

"I would say promotional work. I went from a couple nights a week to almost every night." Daniellé explained.

"The guy from the other state and town was twenty or so years older than your manager. Oh, and he had died a few years back. That bothers me since I can't find multiple people by that name. It's not a common name like John Smith or something." Gabriel concluded.

Daniellé also told that a roommate of hers had told her that the manager's names were not the ones they told the models. Gabriel asked if she knew their names, and she explained about the discussion with Rana and Imogen.

"So, just with what I have collected. You are living in a house with other girls that are being fired, running off with guys, quitting randomly, or running away while others randomly show up the next day. You just so happen to have spare room? The people in charge of the house are undetectable and questionably traceable. You have night gigs that help pay for what rent between twenty or more people for a three-bedroom place? Something is up that is not right. They are making a dishonest fortune off you all at the very least, but the fact that these girls just-? You see what I am saying?" Gabriel's voice was stressed like a big brother.

Gabriel's words made all the sense in the world to Daniellé now, but she never saw the subtle signs.

It was like falling into a camouflaged trap in the woods.

It is like boiling a frog.

They never feel the water temperature rising.

It happened too slowly.

Every action was precise.

Daniellé's head began spinning.

They were like snipers from a distance, and the red dot was unseen in her red hair. She collapsed slowly onto to roof almost as if the shot had been fired.

"What do I do?" Daniellé began crying as she asked for advice.

"Be smart. Get out of there. Personally, I would leave as soon as you can. Even if this just a bad company looking for a buck, they do not have your best interest at heart. And I think it is much more than that. Truly Daniellé, I think what they are selling and their motives…they are not in your favor. I think you are part of something entirely different than what you came to New York for. I love you, and I do not want to see you in any danger." Gabriel advised.

"What about the others?" Daniellé asked. "Should I tell them?"

"I don't know, Daniellé. Possibly? How did they react to these other girls? We need to get you home though. That is the priority." Gabriel said, his voice full of concern.

"I know. I will leave tonight. Sneak out after one of those promotional gigs when they don't know. They have been with us a lot more since Rana left. They're trying to not let us out of their sight." Daniellé said confidently.

"Okay. I will investigate this more. I can call a few friends. Let me know if you need anything." Gabriel assured her it was going to be okay before hanging up.

It was not enough though. The redhead folded her knees against her chest and curled position as she cried to the echoes of cars on the streets and Latin music from the neighbors.

She was going to allow herself these few minutes to be weak.

She was going to allow herself this time to be afraid.

She was weak and moronic.

From small town to big city, she had been lied to, betrayed, and treated like anything but a person.

At least, that is how she saw herself now.

She called more people she believed could have answers. Either they did not, or her calls went to voicemail. She had never felt so…alone.

Truly, she was just a small-town girl in too deep and just now realizing what it meant in that classic New York City saying. Thing is, she was not making it in New York, but if she did not leave soon, she was not going to make it anywhere.

Daniellé composed herself as she entered the door to the house. Kathleen stood on the other side of the door. She was dressed in all black with heels poked out of her bag. It was the classic attire for a casting call. Daniellé's eyes felt relief when she crossed the rushed model's path.

"We need to talk. I've learned more. You know the conversation from the subway between you and the others? I had someone look into it." Daniellé's words were rushed trying to get to the point.

"Really? Can it wait? I do not want to be late." Kathleen looked half concerned and half nonchalant.

"No. It really is important. I will walk with you to wherever. Just let me grab my purse." Daniellé insisted.

"I really do not have time." Kathleen protest as Daniellé rushed to get her bag.

Kathleen had already made it to the bottom of the staircase as Daniellé opened the door. She followed her down the steps.

Daniellé went on. "We need to leave. Tonight. Bring no attention to us. Listen. Damn it! Listen to me." Daniellé's voice broke in her plea to Kathleen.

She began showing anything she could from Gabriel's research and she shared what Rana had said.

"You've talked to Rana?" Kathleen inquired.

"Not since that day. But that is not the point." Daniellé continued.

Why have I not heard from Rana, yet? She said she would call? Daniellé thought.

"What do you want me to think?" Kathleen said it a bitter voice. "That what you are saying is true? You know they told me not to listen to you, right? I do not want to ruin my chances for this audition. I will look at this all later." Kathleen's voice was not so kind and gentle anymore.

Kathleen's time in New York was hardening her, and the GAL agency's toxic words were causing Daniellé's attempt to educate her to backfire.

"Look, please. I had someone investigate this for me. It is the only thing that makes sense. And now, people are just gone. Try calling Rana. Texting her. I don't understand why she doesn't reply. Please, listen." Daniellé's face ran with tears as she spoke.

Kathleen began to take Daniellé seriously as she suggested. "How about I just share this with the team? They will have answers. Maybe even know why the others aren't answering?"

Daniellé placed her hand on Kathleen's forearm.

"If this is the reality of the situation how can we do that? All I am trying to do is shared what I learned. Either way, I am leaving. Something is not right here." Daniellé's tears followed her words.

If Kathleen told those people, she was terrified of what management could do or even who they really were.

"Okay. I won't. I will have my dad look at this. Was it really that bad? I mean, yeah, nothing seems to be going well." Kathleen's voice became more worried. Daniellé could see her recalling all the latest events.

"Okay." Daniellé nodded as she spoke. "Let me know what your dad finds out?"

"Of course." Kathleen nodded yes as she turned to leave again. She turned back though with a horrid expression. "Can you go ahead and send me what your friend found out?"

"Sure." Daniellé agreed. "The guy's name is Gabriel Thomas."

"The Gabriel Thomas?" Kathleen asked.

"Yeah, he ran for mayor a few years back." Daniellé told her.

Kathleen's expression was more serious now that she knew Daniellé's source. "I will call my dad on the train." Kathleen's words sounded like she was talking more to herself than Daniellé.

"Okay. Good luck." Daniellé said.

"Thanks." Kathleen said. Her voice sounded automated as she looked lost in thought.

That was such a mistake. I will leave as everyone is sleeping -with or without her. Hopefully she will tell me if she finds out anything else. Daniellé thought.

Daniellé decided the best way to get out of this was to lay low. She was going to go to the promo tonight, and in that witching hour of returning home, she would pack what she could carry and get the Hell away from this place. The local coffee shop was a good place to calm here mind with a lavender latte.

I will just go there and focus. She convinced herself.

Daniellé was not shocked that Kathleen did not believe their prior conversation until she mentioned of Gabriel. She would have thought it was crazy too. That is why Daniellé was so adamant about researching everything when Rana had freaked out and the girls on the subway had mentioned their thoughts on these strange events.

These were Gabriel's facts. Daniellé had called up a trusted friend and mentor to do the research. In a matter of a few hours, he could tell Daniellé that there was no official business under the name of GAL agency, no official address connected to their business, and that the people she knew as Caleb and Richmond were not legit. Perhaps, they were not those people at all. Perhaps, their names were, say Matthew and Lucas, and they were related. Perhaps, they were not just distantly related, but Matthew and Lucas were brothers or cousins. Perhaps, this was not a modeling agency at all. Perhaps, these people were selling something that Daniellé or the others had never intended. It explained everything and nothing at the same time. In fact, the only real answer Daniellé understood was that she needed to get the hell away from this place.

Section Three: Red Flags

If you hang a red flag from the top of a flagpole against a clear blue sky, its contrast will be bold. No doubt the redness will be apparent. No doubt anyone will be able to see it from a distance or up close. This is obvious, but if you hang the same flag in the pitch-black darkness of night, no one will see it.

Red flags do not become redder over time. They remain as they always were. The true obstacle is to know if it is a true red flag flowing from the flagpole. For Daniellé her personal flag was white, but in the darkness, she was not seeing the red warning sign hanging in the darkness.

Commencing Eventuality

Daniellé remembered a statistic from one of her classes back home: two out of three rapes go unreported every year in America. It was something like less than 3% of the prosecuted perpetrators spend a day in jail. At first, Daniellé did not understand why only 3%.

Why did the victims not say something?

Why did the victims not pursue justice?

It was horrifying to think about, let alone share, but does that mean the victims never reported it? Back then, the thought circled in Daniellé's mind after the `professor's speech. It lingered in her mind the day after too. How could two-thirds of these victims just completely miss the opportunity for justice –or at least for potential healing.

Daniellé thought about the helplines provided for victims of assault. She figured that if these rapes went unreported to the police, they must be recorded somewhere. So, perhaps, helplines provided a haven to some extent. They are often operated by past victims of these cruel circumstances. So, do people call helplines when they feel like they can't find, or trust help elsewhere? It made sense to her.

When someone cannot prove it; they may not report it. When the person is your boss, family, wealthy man, a celebrity, or just has the authority over you, they may be terrified. If you are not as important as them, it may seem hopeless. None of this makes it right, but this is not a just world, and good does not always win.

Daniellé thought deeper about this topic over the next few days.

What if they say it doesn't count?

Daniellé researched the definition of rape online —unlawful sexual activity under threat. It was broad, and somehow different from sexual assault. It was vaster than the consensus of society's determination of the word. Rape, a word that causes the body to automatic shutter, was not just vaginal and penial. It included foreign objects, body parts, even something as vague as a sexual touch.

She pondered deeper. *What if the person says it isn't true?*

What if they call the victim a liar, or worse yet, say they wanted it?

What if either way the victim loses?

Something was wrong.

She could feel *some things*.

She could think *some things*. She could not move *hardly anything*.

It was not that the room was spinning, but the sensation of her high-heeled covered feet pressed against the nightclub floor was minimal. No. The room was not spinning, but everything was in slow motion as if from a distance. Like the fog drifting off a Maine rocky coast line, Daniellé was unconnected from her surroundings.

He was fully aware though.

Moments before, for the first time Daniellé was given permission to leave the group without accompaniment. It was a new event spot, and when Daniellé entered with the others she missed seeing the name of the venue. The only real difference about this place she noticed was that the lights flashed blue and green instead of white or gold like the other promotional spots.

She knew it was odd Zane, Caleb, and Richmond had let her go off alone to the unisex restroom. It was a clear violation of the *ten commandments* provided weeks earlier. She liked the idea of being away from them, and she had spent all evening deep in thought of when she arrived back to the model house. She had already packed her suitcase without anyone noticing.

She had been ready to get the hell away from this place.

Until now.

Over the course of the last twenty minutes Daniellé started feeling more and more nauseated. She knew it was most likely due to the enormous amount of stress and worry she was under, so she had stayed hydrated while snacking on almonds. Too hydrated, she was already on her fifth bottle of water since walking into the place. Nonetheless, she felt like vomiting, so she asked to leave the table. It was still odd that the manager told her she could handle it on her own by this point. It was always about the numbers with them. They needed to have a full table always, and with so many girls now gone, the rules became stricter about restroom breaks and nights off. Daniellé thought she could handle it on her own. She even felt a little bit like a badass as she weaved through the crowd. The loud rap music and darkness gave her a false sense of empowerment. People tend to forget that the worse type of events typically happen in the dark.

Caleb had once said, "Not everyone in the city is *good natured*. Trust no one — especially strangers."

At the time it sounded like the classic parent speech given to a wide-eyed child. But, perhaps, they just knew all too well of the dangers that lurked everywhere. Perhaps, the "no one" Caleb referred to was someone all the models knew — not a stranger at all.

Daniellé wished she could say something. She wished she could run away or raise a fist to fight. She wished the lights of the club would shine this way. She wished a camera would angled in her direction or that a bouncer was near. She wished she knew how this even happened. One moment she was exiting a dim restroom the next, she was in the dark. She had not been drinking alcohol. She has not been drinking anything but water. She had not even really spoken to anyone after the conversation with Kathleen. Her plan was to leave while everyone else was sleeping. She had only wanted to get away.

It did not last long. Maybe, it was ten minutes at the most.

After she felt rough hands sliding up her black skirt, Daniellé's mind entered a survival numb state. It was almost like her body played possum. She was not numb. Daniellé felt pressure from every angle. It was like being imprisoned in Hell, but not in fire and flame, his Hell was full of bitter, frigid isolation. She lived there for these long minutes. But he did not stop. He did not look into her eyes. His face pressed against her breasts. That was where he lived for those minutes. During the whole time the only word she thought she heard him say was cherish. It was not the traditional Webster definition. Perhaps, Daniellé could be thankful for that one detail. But no matter the method, it was anguish.

From the distance, people may have assumed they were just having *fun*. Maybe, the nightlife party-goers alleged this was what she *wanted*. How would they know any different when she could not scream while her body was against this wall motionless? He hovered over her, hiding her reaction from the world, and even if he hadn't, it was too dark to see the tears rolling down her pink cheeks.

She was a pawn in his chess game. He trapped her completely — checkmate. She never asked her roommate about what she saw that day in the model house. She did not want to offend or cause a fight if it was consensual. She did not want to embarrass her if it was not. It was such a sensitive topic, and the girl had acted fine afterwards. The more time passed, the more she thought she had just walked in on two people having fun. Daniellé had tried to make herself available if the girl wanted to talk to anyone, but she was not close to her anyways. The chances of her speaking to Daniellé about it were slim to none, but she made herself available. All either of them knew about other another came from the daily gossip in the house. They could not even really call one another friends.

Maybe this was deserved. Maybe, this was karma. Maybe, some roommate of hers was watching from a distance thinking the same exact thoughts she had that day. A cosmic joke with no audience to laugh.

He was the first to leave. It was like one final authoritative stab before departure. In some Eastern cultures the person of most importance and prestige leaves first when meetings are over. In olden times persons of prestige ate first and were given all the best servings of the meals. The smallest and most unimportant of the company waited behind, sometimes they were even responsible for the cleanup. Daniellé just kept on leaning against the wall in the dark. After some time had passed she could hear the music more than the thoughts in her head. She could see the people walking in the dark. Slowly, she re-entered reality from the astral plane.

It was not until Kathleen and a Ukrainian-looking model walked close by the restrooms that Daniellé had full control of her legs again. When she reached the blonde Barbie, her face was as horrified as Daniellé's expression. Daniellé did not understand, but Kathleen pulled her past the restroom attendant into a stall before she asked. The Ukrainian was asked to wait until an open stall was available at the door. Kathleen stared at Daniellé silently as the stall shook from the bass of the DJ's music. Barbie stood bemused as Daniellé 's emotions returned like a rushing waterfall.

"What?!" She yelled at Kathleen.

Daniellé recalled the conversation earlier in the day with Kathleen. Daniellé had begged her to leave. Daniellé wanted to get away from this place and these people. She no longer cared about being an IMG or Marilyn model, all she wanted to do diminish out of existence. She did not want to be the girl with the hair on fire. She did not want to be draped on the pages of Bazaar magazine. She did not want to walk the stage of the Victoria Secret modeling annual show. She did not want to *be at all*. Daniellé hated her own existence and physique. She had been a late bloomer. She was the tallest girl in her class by sixth grade, but she was not considered beautiful until her last semester of high school. At that point her friends and family complimented her on her striking features and strong brow game. She would smile sweetly and occasionally it would go to her head.

Beauty was supposed to be a blessing instead it caused her a reckoning. It was this *blessing* that had her convinced fully to die tonight instead meeting the next tomorrow as this supposedly beautiful creature.

"I am sorry." Kathleen cried, Tears running down her cheeks.

At that moment Daniellé realized Kathleen was not here for round two of their debate. The Barbie's eyes shone with terror and fire.

Terror and fire are the chemical mixture in which stains the eyes of its victims. From the moment after their personal hellish event, a feeling of alarm penetrates deep into the location of where the eyes and soul meet. That is how all victims of tragedy possess the eyes of fire. It cannot be hidden in photos or by shutting one's eyes.

It stains.

Call it the mark of life or perhaps, more suitably, the mark of death. Nonetheless, it lives there. Even when terror is weakened by the idea of rescue, safety, or new beginnings, the fire always burns. These two girls stood with matching eyes of fire. The gloss of innocence Kathleen carried about her disappeared. Daniellé's eyes widened as tears rolled downward.

"They were pointing at the others. We aren't supposed to leave the table. I saw it happen again. Then they pointed at me, so I came here. We need to leave." Kathleen revealed.

Daniellé sighed. It could have been much worse for Kathleen. Kathleen could have been her.

"So, we leave." Daniellé's words were firm. "But we do this my way. Okay."

"Okay." Kathleen agreed.

Her mind, heart, and soul shifted without reservation to Daniellé.

"I need you to cover for me. Tell them I am vomiting if they ask. If they don't, then say nothing at all. Stand in the back on the group. Try to be small and hidden, but not too obvious." Daniellé directed.

Kathleen's scared eyes were full of the fear of abandonment. Daniellé's mind was still reeling from earlier, but she had a plan. Perhaps, it would not work, but she had a good idea as she twiddled the single car key in her hand that had made its home in her bra thus far tonight.

"You will see me leave, but I will not leave you." Daniellé assured. "Try to call your parents. Tell them that you need to go home, now, but do not take too long. Honestly, I do not know exactly what is going on anymore."

"Me either." Kathleen said as another tear fell.

"Stop crying and fix up your makeup as best as possible." Daniellé suggested with a soft, motherly tone.

She had no idea why she felt the need to protect Kathleen despite the crude statements she had made. She loved her like she loved her childhood teddy bear or favorite All American Doll. She felt a tethered older sister kind of love for no comprehensible reason.

As Kathleen and Daniellé opened the stall they realized the other model was long gone, and the attendant was frustrated with how long they had been tying up the stall. The irritation remained on seeing the runny mascara of the roommates' faces. Daniellé instructed to Kathleen to walk out first as she made her way to an exit. A sudden gust of cold air consumed her when she found herself outside. Her long legs walked a fast pace as she went towards where she had parked the car. She looked at no one, but tugged on her skirt, pulling it downwards every few steps.

She felt disgusted with herself as men called after her trying to get her attention. It was a true walk of shame.

She started the car and felt a warmth on her shoulders.

I can leave. Right now. I can just go. Daniellé thought.

No one would blame her if she put the pedal to the medal. No one would judge her for wanting to drive far away from this place, this world and *him*. No one, but her.

Daniellé moved the car to a different location. As she turned off the vehicle she thought once more. *I can leave.*

She didn't.

Each step back toward the nightclub made her feel like an innocent witch being sent to the gallows. She begged and pleaded with herself. She did not deserve to hang for this crime, but here she was providing them the rope.

She showed the bouncer her hand and he shone a light over it to see the ultraviolet stamp. It felt like he was personally delivering Daniellé back to her prison. She weaved through the crowd until she stood beside Kathleen. One manager was gone, but Daniellé did not dare look around for the other. She kept her eyes locked forward as she and Kathleen stood shoulder to shoulder for the duration of the shift.

Kathleen's father had booked her a hotel for the night. Kathleen was kind enough to share it with Daniellé. It was not far enough from the model townhouse for Daniellé's piece of mind, but it was something. It was either be a few minutes down the street or sleep on the street. Daniellé smiled thankfully at idea of sticking together. Perhaps, Kathleen did see Daniellé as a friend or Kathleen was just too scared to be alone. The redhead did not really care what the reasoning was behind the gesture, she was just satisfied with the result: they were away from those people.

It was a typical hotel room with oddly red patterned carpet and a white bed with white sheets. There was a small dark colored oak writing desk in the corner by a wide window. The curtains draped down to the floor in a light earthy green shade. Both sides of the bed had nightstands with tacky wholesale lamps. Other than the basics the only other asset a beige wide seat sofa chair. It was nearly 5:00 a.m., and this place was heaven for the girls. Sure, they were still sharing a room, but compared to sharing a room with five or six girls, it was a spacious and refreshing treat.

Daniellé striped the top sheet from the bed and a white overstuffed pillow from the bed. Tossing them onto the beige chair, she asked if Kathleen wanted to use the restroom first before she showered. Daniellé knew she wanted a long, almost burning shower, to remove *him* from her. She knew better than to shower after an event like this, and the correct thing to do is go to a hospital. The correct thing to do is seek out help. Something in her mind would not share what happened even with Kathleen. It was like he had left her with some type of psychological landmine. When Daniellé left her trance state, she saw that Kathleen had already crawled into bed. Still wearing makeup and her evening dress. She looked peaceful fast asleep. The poor girl had been too exhausted to even lift the comforter. She just laid down on the dressed bed. Daniellé walked over to the other side of the bed untucking the covers enough to fold them back over and lay them over her Barbie friend.

Fashion Affliction

Daniellé put on the extra security lock for the room door after slipping the "Do Not Disturb" sign on the handle. The two of them deserved a little peace and quiet even for a few hours. Daniellé removed a tee shirt and pair of shorts from her suitcase. Making her way to the restroom, Daniellé turned on the faucet to the shower. As the water began to heat, she closed the door.

She refused to make visual contact with the any mirrors as her outfit fell to the floor. She only stood in the shower for a moment before she sat on its bright white floor. Her chin rested on her knees as her arms wrapped around legs. From the corner of her eyes she saw a flow of blood reach the drain of the shower. The burning heat of the water turned her light skin flushed pink. In her college health classes Daniellé learned of the bacteria transfer between human beings that resulted from intercourse of any sort. The studies explained how your partner's DNA could combine with yours. After a cycle of regeneration and replication, the other person's DNA would incorporate entirely with yours. Essentially, the two people quite literally become a part of one another. *He* could, possibly, be a part of her from this point forward. Whether physical marked or not, he would be forever with her -tarnished with the haunting memory he gave her.

Her body shook as she stared at the wall in the shower. Re-entering a trance, her eyes faced toward the white tile of the lower half of the shower, but all she saw was the same event replaying in her mind.

Her mind was lost in a rapid cycle of disorganized thought. *How? I didn't drink alcohol.*

Daniellé remembered more from that college class on rape. Most just get away with it.

They can't help me. I can't prove it. No cameras. No lights. I can't face him. I got to get away. These type of people…I can't. I can't tell my parents. She thought about how the very thought of this would destroy her mother and father.

The judgement of her family. They could not know. This was to be her own pain. This was to be her one unfashionable mistake. This was her fashion affliction. Her soul was falling more into despair as the flowing water went from hot to cold. Daniellé scrubbed her arms and legs with a Dial bar of soap. When the coldness became unbearable she stretched out her arm to pull the lever to the off position. Instead of exiting, Daniellé just stayed on the shower floor.

Daniellé's thoughts raced. *I don't know who they even are, but they know everything about me. I have no money to get home. I don't even really know where I am at. Gabriel? I can't tell him what happened.*

Daniellé did not cry. Her composure was the last bit of control she possessed. If she began to cry, all control would be lost. Not breaking down gave her a chance to get home without making any dumb decisions. Her head began spinning as if she was hungover. Stress or whatever had affected her mind earlier was being processed by her liver. Standing slowly, she made her way to the bathroom sink to drink. Still avoiding seeing herself in the mirror, she slipped on her clothes. Slowly, Daniellé curled up into a ball on the beige chair. Her phone said that it was close to 6:00 a.m. placing it on the charger, she shut her eyes. It was as if the entire world dissolved in a matter of seconds as she found herself asleep. That night she had no dreams- just blackness.

Daniellé woke at 8:00 a.m. as the light peeped through the curtains hitting her face. Kathleen was comfortably still asleep. The model still needed about a million more hours of sleep, but Daniellé knew she needed to focus on the next course of action. Checkout was in two hours, and she had no plan on what to do next. Kathleen's parents had already booked her a flight home. She must have been better off financially than she let on to afford a sudden ticket out of New York City. Daniellé did not have such a luxury. If she was not willing to call her family for help, perhaps, Gabriel would have a better idea. He had mentioned having friends in the city and was always resourceful. Daniellé picked up her phone to see if he had messaged her back. The phone alerted her of several other messages and calls instead. Most the missed calls were not from numbers she recognized, but she did have a few messages from GAL asking where she was.

"Damn it." Daniellé said loudly enough to wake Kathleen.

"Huh. What?" Kathleen muttered as she woke up.

"Do you have any calls or messages?" Daniellé inquired.

Kathleen gave Daniellé a concerned look as she picked up her phone. Her eyes puzzled.

"Yeah." Kathleen said as she scrolled through her phone. "I have to get ready. I need to leave for my flight in like thirty minutes," she said.

"Okay, yeah." Daniellé turned on the lights to the room as Kathleen headed toward the restroom.

Daniellé turned off her phone to avoid any more stressful calls. She dressed and braided her hair into a bun. It was hard to hide her firetruck colored hair, but a bun and hood was the best option. She was not sure if she needed to hide, but she also knew she was not out of the woods yet. When Kathleen was ready, the two girls made their way downstairs for breakfast. They choose a corner table both facing the wall. Food did not appeal too much to Daniellé, but Kathleen seized the opportunity. Instead Daniellé stuffed her bag with some nonperishable items for later.

"My taxi is here." Kathleen said. "Are you going home?"

"Yeah. Figuring it out." Daniellé said.

"Okay. Well, let me know?" Kathleen asked. "And, I am sorry."

"Don't be. They were messing with our heads." Daniellé looked at the ground as she said that last sentence.

Kathleen grabbed her suitcase and waved goodbye.

Daniellé was alone again. She got up for a cup of coffee as she contemplated what she would say to Gabriel. She reviewed what she knew, which in all reality was not enough. Her mind raced. *The new business. Connected to the old escorting business. Connected to modeling. Probably wanted good looking young women. Odd names. No names?* She gulped at a thought which shook her further.

They had offered the models the house money to recruit new girls. At the time it had seemed like a great way to make some extra cash when wallets were bare. Helping other inspiring models reach their dreams sounded like a great way to give back. Leaping up from her chair, Daniellé hovered over the trash can of the dining hall, vomiting.

She ignored the alerts coming out of her pocket as she messaged her friends.

Don't cry. She told herself.

The only thing that mattered right now was getting home.

Daniellé's phone rang again with the strange number. For a moment she thought it could be Gabriel or even one of the other models. Daniellé answered, but she did not say a word.

The other person on the line did not speak either. It was a cold, bitter silence. If it had been Gabriel, he would have spoken immediately. Daniellé did not know if she was in a silent stand-off with a roommate, a previous roommate, GAL, or even *him*. It went on and on, but Daniellé felt an invisible pressure preventing her from hanging up. Instead the other line clicked off, ending the call. Daniellé's mind was frozen. She watched hotel members enter and leave the dining hall, not sure what to do next. Grabbing her things, she flipped her hood back over her head as she headed toward the exit of the hotel. She did not have any sort of solid game plan except to head toward the subway and go in the direction of the airport or any direction away from here. The streets were less crowded here and cars did not pass nearly as often as the back to back traffic of Manhattan.

It did not take long to realize that she had no idea if a subway would even be close to this area of town. Daniellé was beginning to feel lost. She had walked ten, fifteen, or maybe even twenty minutes. It was time to turn back towards the hotel.

Only thing was, there was no time to turn back.

Models Stop Traffic • 180

Eschec mat. (Checkmate)

Buy Out

It was dark, the worse type of dark, the type of dark in which any source of light burned the eyes with its brightness, the type of dark that feels cold like the shock of an ice pack placed on the skin too quickly, the type of dark where someone feels motionless and unconnected with all the senses, the type of dark that Lucifer says is his version of heaven, but it's hell. It was that type of dark the Daniellé found herself in now.

There was no way to tell the time of day or how long she had been knocked out. There was no way to discover where she was or why this was happening. She tried to move. She was barely coherent enough to realize her hands were connected to the bedpost above her. Her left shoulder was locked in place causing striking pain. She felt what could have been a shirt, scarf, or even the bed sheet.

When she opened her eyes, they burned from the runny mascara, the swollen aftermath of tears she could not recall shedding. Her mind was hazy from the possible medical cocktail in her system. Daniellé was someone who rarely, and by rarely two times in her life, drank anything stronger than two ounces of red wine in one sitting. So, whatever had taken residence in her body had hit for its maximum effect. Her brain felt immense pain and a topsy-turvy sensation. She was not utilizing it for any sort of thought, and it still was enough to make her beg for the return of unconsciousness. Her only bearable sense was her hearing. She could hear an assortment of moans, squeals, and conversation in nearby rooms. She knew she was not alone in this dark area. She could hear the close rattle of someone perhaps no more than a few feet from her. Her unknown kindred soul's voice was weak. That was, if she was not imagining it or if it wasn't some a guardian angel. For all she could tell, the devil himself was providing these soft whimpers just to toy with her mind.

"Please. I'm not good." The kindred soul whimpered.

The model's head was splitting from a migraine. She tried to speak, but it was as if she had forgotten language. It was impossible for her to even know if her mouth was open for words. Instead, she closed her eyes again to hear more of her surroundings. She filtered out the sounds beyond the rattling and shifting of bed frames in hopes of tuning into the distant conversation. It sounded like English, but not an American dialect.

Daniellé tried sorted as best as she could through her memories. She searched. She filtered. The only words that came to her head were *baby* and *girl*. No meaning would attachment to them. Instead of focusing on herself, she listened harder.

Who are those voices? She had as her first complete thought.

Daniellé could not remember the countries, let alone dialects. Then the language shifted. English words transitioned into something else entirely. They transitioned into something she knew the meaning of, but unable to detect why she knew. Her head made slow, low range nods as she followed the syllables of the words. Another ten minutes passed until she connected the first word to a language. She let the word repeat in her head. She let it repeat until this word was the only word that held any meaning in her life. And once she heard her mind speak it twenty, thirty, maybe even forty times. She said it.

Out loud she said, "Heures (Hours)." Her voice faded in repetition of the word.

"Heures. Heures. Heures."

As her head fell back into what felt like a concrete mattress she weakly said. "French for Heures." Her pain tolerance collapsed again at the expense of her survival.

Don't Caress Fire

Caressing is a form of tenderness toward the object or person in hand. It is a gentle light loving touch throughout the area typically skin or hair. It is done with care and slowly with intent. It is meant to be…appreciated as moments of adoration. It is meant to show care and indebtedness. It can cause the subject's body to relax or tense at the precise strokes up and down a body. Sometimes it is followed by kisses, and sometimes nibbles or playful bits. All to create something along the lines of arousal and longing for more; to make the subject or person receiving the attention long for it or accept the arousal openly.

Perhaps, that was the man's thoughts when his body loomed above the weak-limbed model. Her eyes were blinded by cloth while her mouth bound by something similar. Her body tensed at these touches, but not out of excitement or anticipation. These touches were very unwelcome, but her futile struggle was only a game to the caresser. He was slow and deliberate, but without an ounce of genuine care. Instead, this caress felt like hate. As if her body was placed beside the flames of a fire. She felt burned.

It was his game.

A game he would win, and she would lose.

A Model's "Dream"

Daniellé tossed and turned as her body fought off the influence of drugs in her system. Her body ached from a previous beating. The pain resonated throughout her muscles. Less than an hour ago she had bitten a man that came to *get off* at her expense. The man was larger than her in all ways, and Daniellé was tied to a bed post, but there was no way she was going to let any man take advantage of her again without a fight. She had already failed twice, but she still fought as the cloth choked her muffled screams.

When he laid his body on top of hers she used both knees to strike his genitals. With full force a head-butt caused them both an instant headache. The fight was worth it to her, even if Daniellé experienced the beating of a lifetime consequently. The infuriated man left her wrists tied to the bedpost as he dragged her body off the bed. He kicked her ribs and chest. He avoided her face to not reduce her marketable value. In human trafficking everything has value with the most coveted prizes being virgins and little boys. She cried barren on the floor, but she won this time. Daniellé had killed his sexual appetite.

"Bitch." He swore at her.

He held his head as he left. Daniellé's body throbbed as she passed out. Now unconscious her mind escaped reality as she now found herself in a dream state.

Models Stop Traffic • 186

Daniellé stood at the front of a room full of staring eyes. She recognized some as friends and family, but others were complete strangers. Behind her was eleven coffins. Photos next to each of them displayed images of her New York City roommates, and the one directly behind her was a picture of herself. The audience seemed to be waiting for a eulogy speech. She cleared her throat.

"Before we can break barriers, we must break what currently stands. Sometimes reality is the only true perception. New York City made my dreams feel like reality, and even though I worked hard each day, I wonder if it all was just a dream. This dream was our lives. Please know, we fought. We were strong." Daniellé said to the crowd in front of her.

Daniellé was right. They were all strong…She was strong. The first time she knew of her own inner strength and resilience in the modeling industry was when she was a freshman in college. It was Valentine's Day, and her boyfriend, Neil Muir, did not visit because of a two-hour drive fraternity party he wanted to attend. As a result, a friend of Daniellé's, named Andrew Sherri, asked her to spend the evening together as friends. Daniellé agreed, and they arranged to go see a movie.

Daniellé had wanted to clear everything with Neil first, but when she called him to ask permission, he dismissed her. She felt like he was indifferent, and it was enough to make her feel unimportant. Daniellé was angry her boyfriend did not want to spend Valentine's together, but Daniellé's Valentine's day luck had never been good in the past so, she was not entirely surprised.

Their conversation had been like a ping-pong match with Daniellé sending volleys of caring and Neil sending back serves of nonchalance. Neil had drained her emotionally, and an emotionally beaten down Daniellé had retreated as she hung up the phone. Shortly after her phone rang again showing Andrew's number. She explained how she would be spending Valentine's night alone.

Andrew was one of her fellow theatre-loving acting friends. While Daniellé preferred the camera, Andrew loved the stage. They had met the first semester of college and remained close throughout the winter break.

"Well, we will just have a chill friend night." Andrew said.

Daniellé questioned if Andrew was into girls or was just saving himself for the right one. She adored Andrew in a cute puppy way, but she did not want to look like a cheater by going out with another man on Valentine's Day. Even if her boyfriend did choose a frat party over seeing her.

"I don't know, Andrew. Don't you think it would appear like I'm being unfaithful? I know we're just friends, but still. It would look bad." Daniellé explained.

"Would it help if I asked him if it was okay?" Andrew laughed.

"Actually, yes. Maybe? That would help a lot." Daniellé answered sarcastically.

Next thing she knew, Neil had told Andrew he did not care if her took Daniellé out to a movie night.

Daniellé was angry that Neil answered Andrew, but still would not return her phone call.

What type of boyfriend doesn't care if his girlfriend goes out with another guy on Valentine's Day? Daniellé thought.

Andrew picked Daniellé up around 7:30 p.m. for the 8:15 p.m. movie. The plan was to see the movie Breaking Day -with a running time of nearly four hours. It was Andrew's choice, but looking back she really wished she would have objected. It was the only movie Daniellé had ever fallen asleep while watching. It was freezing outside when they left the theater. The conversation was light-hearted as Andrew teased her about falling asleep.

"That bad, eh?" He laughed as he opened the glass door.

"It was awful!" Daniellé's smile was half embarrassed and half trying to wake up still.

"I liked it a lot." He rebutted.

Andrew explained why he thought the movie was amazing. She clearly disagreed as she tucked at her pink dress and white cardigan for warmth, but after all his kindness, and the fact Daniellé was not at home in tears, she decided to let him have this one. Andrew noticed Daniellé's shiver as they continued the walk down Jay Street.

"Did you not tell me you were a track star back in high school? Racing sprints all the way to state?" Andrew was trying to get her mind off the cold.

She entertained him with a giggling laugh, "Yes, I was always the only white girl in the 200-yard dash at regional and state finals."

Andrew's eyes lit up like the Christmas decorations in the city in which had not taken down the December light's yet.

"Well, how about a race to the car then?" He suggested trying to antagonize her.

"I am wearing black heel boots, Andrew!" Daniellé said laughing.

He continued to make fun of her, and after he flashed a quick wink at he took off in full sprint. Daniellé found herself darting toward the car at full speed quickly passing him. The poor girl did not see the unmarked construction zone leading into the underground of the city. Falling into the hole, she face-planted against the concrete. Her pearl necklace busted into pieces. The pain was immense as she landed in the cold underground. Her head was spinning as she noticed people, including Andrew surrounding her from above. Raising her head from the cold rocky surface, she wanted to close her eyes and return to the rock.

She quickly went into shock. The damage done was far beyond the power of Band-Aids and isopropyl alcohol to fix. With hands presented in a starting push-up position, she felt the enormous throbbing of her mouth and chin. Like most people might, Daniellé clenched her teeth in a wince of pain.

Her eyes widened.

Daniellé's teeth refused to clench down as she winced. In their defense, they could not clench down. Daniellé's front teeth had taken up a new address along with the pearls of her broken necklace leaving Daniellé's pointy tongue poking through a newfound hole. These are the moments where she knew karma had caught up with her. Sure, Daniellé was vain, but most girls have some degree of vanity in their blood or at least in their makeup bag.

Daniellé cursed, "Hey God, I know you are up there. Did you really think this was necessary?"

Back then, she did not think God really liked talking with her. To Daniellé God was more of the silent parent type who wanted to teach her lessons.

"Those were her teeth that shattered!" Roared an unfamiliar voice in the distance.

Yes, someone was highlighting Daniellé's reality like newspaper headlines. She wanted to just lay there until this night turned into day. Even though Daniellé was only down for five minutes, she could envision completing the rest of her days on this construction zone concrete. Daniellé removed herself from the situation in her mind to see how this scenario might look to a bystander. Here it is Valentine's night and some random girl is running from a boy at full speed in a pink dress and heel boots. She runs straight into an unmarked construction zone and takes a tumble remaining lifeless at the bottom. Sounds like a perfect day of love.

Andrew, in a frenzy, stood above her.

"Daniellé! Daniellé! Are you alright?!" Andrew frantically started evaluating Daniellé's current health condition.

"That's relative," The broken girl answered.

After helping Daniellé up to her knees, she saw the utter terror reach Andrew's normally calm brown eyes. Daniellé was not sure if she played the role of patient or doctor. She felt the need to take care of him instead. A group of two couples appeared suddenly to help the ill fainted girl from her fall. Daniellé began to lose a lot of blood from the cuts and breaks to her face, collar bone, and arm. The Good Samaritan Act was being applied to the maximum tonight as the unrecognized voices surrounded Daniellé to help.

One voice said, "She's losing a lot of blood."

Another said, "We can take her up to my friend's apartment. He will have things up there."

Daniellé heard Andrew swiping through the concrete rubble as she fainted.

Several minutes later, Daniellé was being lifted to an apartment building across from where she had fallen. It was one of the tallest buildings in downtown, and she saw it almost every day from the outside, but this was her first time inside. Most of the lights were still turned off in the hurry, but the city lamps peaked through the windows providing some amount of illumination. Daniellé leaned against a tall muscular man, in which that made her somehow feel both nervous and safe. Andrew was right behind Daniellé assuring her repeatedly everything would be okay.

"Sure, as Hell, does not feel okay." Daniellé whispered to herself.

The kind strangers guided Andrew and Daniellé to the restroom.

"He must live here. Lucky us." Andrew said hopefully.

"Lucky. Ha." Daniellé scoffed as she winced in pain.

"It will be okay." Andrew assured her.

The restroom was big enough to fit Andrew and Daniellé, but no more than them. At eye-level facing Daniellé was an old rusted mirrored medicine cabinet. As she examined herself, she too had seen better days. Her once perfectly curled hair was now decorated with dirt and blood. The T-zone of her face was scraped from the rocky concrete. Her right-front tooth looked like Michelangelo had taken his chisel to the center of it, and her left tooth was completely gone. All in all, Daniellé looked like she had just escaped a Stephen King movie. Tears flooded her eyes as her strength dissipated.

A long piece of torn skin hung from her chin to mid-way down her neck. There was an enormous gash down her jaw, and if it had gone any deeper it would have shown her jawbone. Andrew reached for Daniellé's hand as he saw her take in her updated appearance. She no longer looked like model material with a blood-stained dress and boots.

As a pool of blood developed in the sink, the volume of a decent Blood Bank donation, Daniellé told Andrew she needed scissors, paper towels, and alcohol. One of the unfamiliar Samaritans collected her requests with Andrew. Returning with supplies,

Andrew handed Daniellé scissors trying to politely hide his disgust. He appeared to be next on the fainting list.

Daniellé laughed to lighten the mood, and said, "Well, this will make for quite a story, won't it?

It worked as Andrew slightly smirked. Then Daniellé reached up with the hair trimming scissors to cut the hanging skin from her chin in one quick snip. Andrew turned away with his mouth covered. She wrapped the dead skin in tissue paper and flushed it. Silent tears began forming as she turned toward Andrew.

"I think we should definitely take you to the emergency room now." Andrew announced with a gulp.

They thanked the good Samaritans, and Andrew and Daniellé walked to her car. The temperature no longer bothered them. The two of them were racing in a different way now. Andrew profusely apologized to Daniellé as he began trying to call her parents, best friend, or anyone Daniellé knew better than him. Daniellé realized a harsh reality with every step closer to her car; she would be driving herself to the hospital. Daniellé owned an old beat up manual car. Daniellé knew Andrew did not know how to drive a manual. She was lucky in one way as the local hospitals were only around seven miles away. At least by this time of night, all the singles had drunk their wine and ate their misery in chocolate, and all the couples were, well, occupied.

Hospitals never have available parking. On top of that, hospitals also charge for parking which in Daniellé's opinion was inappropriate. Personally, she thought it should be against the law to charge an injured patient for parking. They were already going to spend an incredible amount of funds on hospital bills. Was it necessary to charge another $5.00 an hour to park, too? Since Andrew and she were poor students they parked at a neighboring closed bank.

They walked. They walked. Then he carried her. Daniellé felt herself losing a lot of blood once again, and thus was close to fainting once more. For some reason, they could not find the Forte Sanders hospital entrance to save her life. As the story went on Daniellé would lose her boyfriend because he cheated on her that night, lose her modeling contract from breaching the self-care clause, and of course lose her teeth.

Daniellé's dream returned her back in front of the funeral crowd. Their eyes still looked at her waiting for a continued speech.

She continued. "We aren't given strength, but we spend each day earning it. Nothing about being kidnapped, raped, beaten, or betrayed by humanity is right. Stolen freedom is not comprehensible until it is your freedom that was robbed. These girls and me, these models and me, are strong. We died strong."

Daniellé looked up at her dream's funeral mourners. They no longer looked inquisitive or sad. Instead they looked demonic. They took pleasure in the pain of the stolen lives. They rose from their seats rushing toward Daniellé in attack. Terrified, Daniellé ran, but it was useless. They had caught her, and she needed more than strength to get out their grip.

The model gasped for breath as Daniellé regained consciousness. Not much time had passed since her beating. She was alone in the darkness. The lack of proper circulation of her now purplish wrists caused agonizing cramps. She found herself soiled and drenched in her own sweat and mixed body fluids. When she looked up she saw her bags were close by, but too far to reach. Reasonably, it could mean she had not been in this place all that long. She was not sure if a short time frame in hell was a good thing or bad. Maybe, this was just the beginning.

Please, just end. Daniellé prayed.

Human

Time Passed.

It had happened again.

At this point Daniellé had a choice. Give up or keep fighting. Was it much of a choice though? If she kept fighting this could…would…kill her. She puzzled at the thought of not knowing if this would be remembered as a valiant fight or just a pity she did not make it? It did not matter either way, no one would remember how it ended. No one was looking for her. No one knew she was even there. She didn't even know where *there* was. She was alone in this place. She was alone in life.

The only chance she had was to rely on herself. So, with those as her facts she decided to take a chance on herself. It would be a haze and, hopefully, later her mind would block it all out as a loss of memory blessing. But if she did whatever it took to escape would she be able to live with everything this place stole from her afterwards? Would her life be worth living afterwards?

She, honestly, did not know.

She did know mere survival was not enough for her life and fighting for survival may just be the cost of living. Nonetheless, Daniellé was only human- a torn, battered, weak little burnt out flame. Yet, if she did not fight, her life would only get worse from here. Her life could end here.

Fight. She decided. *Fight. Survive. Live.*

Her mind would spare her the details of the evils preformed this day, but the floodgate would not stay closed forever. She knew that, but she had made the choice. She would do whatever necessary to get out of this place. She would harm. She would sacrifice. And to her own terror, she would kill for her freedom.

Statistics state escaping a kidnapping is riskier if the person chooses to fight. Other statistics state escape is easier in the first few hours of the kidnapping. If that was not enough to cause confusion, some statistics say the longer the person is held, captive the better their chances of survival. The only true conclusion is that every case is different, and statistics do not really help to save a life.

Time was the friend of her enemy.

In fact, time was not her friend at all. Its hands pointed in all directions, but always unfavorably for the red head. Its digits threw her about in circles, and if she could hear the tick of a clock on a wall it would have the sound of a foe-like laugh. Her cries throughout this day could have been its chimes. Under a man-made influence and their inhumane influence, Daniellé would flounder, but to what end? Daniellé could never pedal faster than time's gears, and the hours were already passing here. The thought of tomorrow's day reaching its bell toll was inviting death to her door one way or another. Daniellé wanted to find hope in today, and a meaning to all this purpose. She prayed to God with all her screams. In this life the only thing she wanted was a hand to hold and a dream to fill. It was all she could ever want or need. But this concept of time, it was Daniellé's oldest of enemies. Now, she greeted it with a silver tongue. She did not know how to win a battle that was already won.

It was just enough time for her life to be forever changed, but not enough time to give up on life. Those first hours had been utter brutality, but Daniellé realized that this was only in preparation of something worse. Not knowing was either a blessing or her potential downfall.

From here, it was all a little blurry. Perhaps, the hardest moments of someone's life are erased from memory for their protection. In a way it can be like memory blocks. Maybe the blows to Daniellé's head had made processing and storing information difficult. No matter the reason, that day, Daniellé decided the only hero she knew was herself. Her captors decided to transport Daniellé to a new location. Her bags were the first to go, and then a man untied one arm at time as she stared dazed at the ceiling above him. The kidnapper manhandling her could not have had police or military training as he tied her hands in front of her body instead of behind. He was not rough on her like the men before or agonizingly gentle like the caresser. If Daniellé went along with the moving process, he would not hurt her.

Transporting a person is supposed to be a quick process. Typically, it requires at least two people. Daniellé's possessions were thrown in the back of a car ahead of her. Her hands remained tied up, and she was poorly blindfolded in the backseat of a vehicle. She could feel the pressure of a large box container near her.

Suitcase? Box? Where are they taking me? Daniellé pondered anxiously.

The redhead acted too weak to walk or fight, but there was not much pretending needed. There was no explanation as to why the lackadaisical transporters did not restrain her further. As the driver started the car and shifted into drive, Daniellé strained to see clearly. She licked and drooled over the cloth covering her mouth to further weaken it. She could tell it was not completely daylight, but not pitch dark. She did not recognize her surroundings until she heard the noise of busy New York streets.

Public place. She thought. *The car is slowing down. Are we at a red light?*

Daniellé screamed as loudly as she could. She banged on windows and doors. She felt the failed attempts of the transporters swinging at her from the front seats. The car was still stopped when one of their doors opened. Quickly, the door at Daniellé's feet opened too, and she desperately kicked the transporter with all her remaining strength. It was hard enough to knock the man backward. Hard enough to give her just enough time. The next instants happened faster than a blink of Daniellé's eyes. She removed the cloth from her face, or perhaps it just fell off naturally from all the salvia. As it fell her first view was of an open door and her satchel directly in front of her. The driver of the car turned his face away from her. Maybe he didn't want to be seen? The model didn't care to see what the driver looked like; all she cared about was getting away. Daniellé grabbed her satchel, but most of its components fell out as she ran.

Somehow…

Some way…

She got a deep cut on the back of her left arm in the process, or maybe it was a reopened cut from earlier? Either way, it was a small price to pay. The transporter found himself frantic by the scene caused. He searched around to see nearby patrons.

If he had grabbed for her, he was too late. Daniellé ran faster than any track record she had ever set. Unlike that awful Valentine's Day, she won. She just kept running and running. It was all she knew to do. Losing garments and other things as she ran, but she refused to stop. It could have been a car backfiring, it could have been a lot of things, but Daniellé could have sworn she heard gunshots behind her. After everything that happened, she could have believed anything. It was the goodness in the world she now doubted. But she would not look back in this desperate moment. She would not stop her life's run. This running was her salvation.

And despite these events, Daniellé's tireless resilience meant she would live.

Section Four: Covergirl

During war, people discover the best and worst qualities of themselves. Yes, they discover their bravery. They discover the soul-connected unity brought by battling side by side. They even find a greater appreciation for the value of life itself.

During a photoshoot, models see the best and worst qualities of themselves. Yes, they discover photoshop does wonders. They discover the unity of a photographer, designer, and makeup or hair artist working side by side. They even find a greater appreciation for the value of art itself.

War unhinges the door of darkness in the human soul. It uncovers the black-and-white line between right and wrong, and it airbrushes it to a gray blur. The mind would like to protect itself from how far one is willing to go to save a life- to save itself, but war will kill as much as it will cause freedom. In everyday society no one would find this acceptable, instead seeing black-and-white of the actions taken as wrong.

The darkness of Daniellé's war would stain her soul from this point forward. It would change everything she knew in black-and-white to gray. Every morning in one way or another, she would wake up to battle. She would wake up to wear makeup and fix her hair as shields. Her darkness could be airbrushed like a Covergirl magazine model's photo, but just like those who do not know photoshop, some do not know war.

Thy Will Be Done

Daniellé held back her tears. Even in the dimming sunlight, her eyes burned from the brightness. The model could tell she was still in the city of dreams, or now more like her nightmares. Her running ended as she reached a more public atmosphere. The skyscrapers hid the clouds and people walked past her as if she was invisible. She never knew the feeling of being invisible in the past, but she welcomed it. This would be the subtle first mark of Daniellé's alternating mindset.

Daniellé thought hard about her next move. She searched for familiarity as she walked through the sea of people. She stumbled about aimlessly until she arrived at a hotel. She walked in, anxious at its open well-lit space.

"Do you have any first aid supplies and a phone?" Daniellé asked the front desk hesitantly.

The clerk left for a moment and returned with an armful of supplies and explained phones were only for hotel guests. He almost looked afraid of Daniellé's appearance as he spoke, but her mind was focused on his hands more than his words.

Safety first then police? She thought.

Her mind played out the scenarios of every time someone called the police in a horror movie. They were always too late. Irreversible damage was already done. The victim should have found safety first then called the police. They might as well be at best forgotten if she flipped the order.

"Thank you. Umm…Where is the restroom?" Daniellé asked very calmly. The hotel clerk just pointed to the left, and Daniellé followed his directions.

When she got inside the restroom she locked the door despite it being a multi-person restroom. She hopped on top of the sink counter. Searching through the medical supplies she found some bandages, alcohol wipes, and gauze. In her ruined satchel she saw her dead phone, passport, and random items like pens and hair ties. Her wallet was missing.

I am either the luckiest person in the world or the unluckiest. She thought.

She noticed the deep but clear wound on the outside of her bicep. For once Daniellé appreciated her larger arms. She cleaned up the blood surrounding the area. It was deep enough to need stitches, but there was no way was she leaving this hotel right now. All she had was dental floss and a sewing needle. She went to work on cleaning and repairing her ruined body. Afterwards, she walked out to thank the hotel clerk, but the hotel team had already switched shifts.

"Hello, ma'am?" Daniellé said sweetly.

"Yes?" A perky short brunette turned to greet her.

"Can I have some extra shampoo?" Daniellé asked politely.

"Oh, sure. Do you need anything else, dear?" She replied.

"Just anything you can spare." Daniellé smiled. "Oh, do you have a phone line by chance?"

"Yes. It is over near the bar area in the office. You will just need your room number and last name to log in." The clerk instructed as she walked to get the requested supplies.

Daniellé waited until the clerk turned the corner to look over the front desk counter.

Anything. Come on. Anything. Daniellé thought as she scanned the desk papers looking for a name of any of the hotel guests.

Nothing.

But behind her a couple walked to the front desk. The hotel clerk returned with a whole pack of hygienic goods. It was quite literally the highlight of Daniellé's day. No, it was the highlight of her whole month. Her hands reached out to receive the fresh goodness.

Soap! Shampoo! Oh my, conditioner! Daniellé's mind cheered.

"Thank you." Daniellé said gratefully as she walked away. She overheard the nice couple providing their information to the clerk.

"Thank you, Tom Shaver." She whispered to herself.

With her new gift bag of goodies, Daniellé walked over to the office area. She sat down with her back facing the wall. Lately, having her back face an open area caused her a lot of anxiety. She felt like an escaped convict. For a few minutes, Daniellé just stared at the phone in wonder.

Who to call?

Her father? No. Gabriel? Maybe? Then the police? She puzzled.

Circumstances had changed from the last time she spoke with Gabriel, but she could still just get out of this Hell. She did not want anyone to know what happened- at least not from her. So, Daniellé made a strategic move. She knew Gabriel would tell her father she needed to go home if she contacted him first. After a quick Google search for his phone number, Daniellé dialed.

But she could not share everything. She wanted to, but her brain wasn't clear enough to form the words. She was a lock safe with an unknown passcode, and this made her a prisoner to herself. So, she shared the parts of her hours without password, and listened to his guidance. Daniellé felt naked in the shadows in attempt to balance one shortening tightrope.

"Uh, Huh. Yeah. I understand." Daniellé nodded as she agreed to Gabriel's instructions.

Gabriel provided the details of getting Daniellé to his friend's house. It would take years for her to tell him everything, and she needed help now. Her only request was to not contact her parents, but she knew he would anyways. Gabriel's instructions to her were clear. Tomorrow, she would travel to the lower half of Brooklyn, a territory she had not ever visited. She would follow the route given to her by Gabriel that would lead her to a purple townhome belonging to a Broadway singer and award-winning filmmaker. There, she would be safe until a flight could be arranged to take her home. It was a small journey, but it still was hard for Daniellé to accept.

Would it be better to travel now or wait? Was she better hidden in daylight or night fall? She worried.

Now, Daniellé knew true monsters lurked the streets of the City of Dreams. She did not want to even go out past 6:00 p.m. She felt exhausted. Tomorrow, she would leave. She left the office area and walked to the lounge area of the hotel. Now, her heart had calmed down, she was able to take in the beauty of the white marble floors and red draping curtains. Classical piano and violin music played from the overhead speakers, but few attendees occupied the bar or tables in the room. In one corner was a dark lavender crescent-shaped couch facing the corner of the room. One would think it would be for individuals looking for a little bit more seclusion in the room.

Daniellé walked over to her new-found haven. As her hand grazed over its surface, she felt sensual energy within it. As she was seated the pressure points of her body collapsed into relaxation. It was a welcoming sensation.

Hours passed.

After the lounge closed Daniellé worked her way back to the stall at the back of restroom. She pushed away all the memories of microbiology class as she sat on the floor leaning her back against the wall of the stall. It took far longer to relax in the bathroom than it did on the couch, but Daniellé managed to fall back asleep. She whispered a small lullaby to herself to prevent the nightmares.

"Little love. The one that came from above. Let your mind go still. And always remember, thy will." Daniellé's songbird voice quieted as she repeated the lyrics.

Acknowledgements

Time is always closer than being just around the bend. It is quicker than my hands typing, "A Model's Dream" on the keyboard. As birthdays flew by so did the ones in my story drift away to their own paths. Time and change partnered commencing eventuality, and with that, all I know is to find peace instead of the constant flight or fight mode. My brave, glamorous sisters I met on this long Manhattan island, the ones who experienced the insanity of these quick changes, I will be our voice. Please know, we've only just begun the fight. To puppy, now and forever, though I am only human, I will handle the backfire. You gave me the patience, financial support, and availability of time to sort through my fashion affliction and write this book. To my parents, please know all your sacrifices have helped me become the woman I am today. Thank you, mother for always making sure I received a journal for Christmas and thank you father for never doubting I could accomplish even the most seemingly impossible goals. Thank you to the one I can only define as wildfire for uplifting me when submitting to publishers. Your mother would be so proud of your pouring out of kindness and protective instincts. And lastly, I thank the beautifully made and elite one who helped me realize these red flags made me capable to help others. I thought they would define me as broken, weak, and damaged, but you changed my mindset and helped me find my passion purpose. You show me off like a lighted, magnifying mirror, and make me not afraid to hear someone call my name. You are an inspiration way beyond the walls of Elite Foundation as a global light upon this world. With all my heart, thank you all for the love you have given me, and with that I share this story. And dare I say it, "Lights. Camera. Action!"

AUTHOR: AIRICA D KRAEHMER

Did you know Models Stop Traffic was originally named Fashion Affliction? Coming home in tremendous pain, Airica journaled hoping to alleviate her emotions. She did not write in chronological order of events, but instead in accordance to what was weighing on her mind. She called the collections the afflictions her fashion industry dream, thus the name Fashion Affliction.

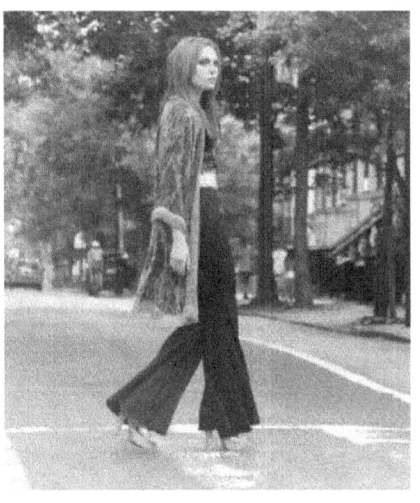

Models Stop Traffic developed when she stumbled upon an old photo of her crossing the street for a fashion print shoot.

When she returned home her troubles did not end, but instead she battled both external and internal conflicts with the events of New York. This aftermath has inspired her to continue writing about the effects of trauma in the sequel of Models Stop Traffic.

Today, Airica's life is heading in an upward and onwards direction. She is now an internationally bestselling author, bachelor's graduate of the University of Tennessee, and is seeking to help bring awareness and eradicate human exploitation. Shockingly, the past has not defined her future as she still can be found on a magazine cover or on the television screen.

She fully believes models can indeed stop traffic.

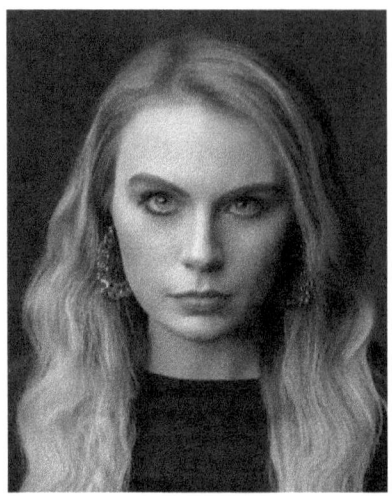

Contact Information:

http://airicakraehmer.com

Social Media:

IMDb: imdb.me/airicakraehmer

Instagram:

https://www.instagram.com/airicakraehmer/

Facebook:

Models Stop Traffic: https://www.facebook.com/modelsstoptraffic/

Airica Kraehmer: https://www.facebook.com/airicakraehmer/

Elite Foundation: https://www.facebook.com/EliteFundsFreedom/

www.ingramcontent.com/pod-product-compliance
Lightning Source LLC
Chambersburg PA
CBHW071529220526
45469CB00003B/697